FAITH UNDER FIRE

FAITH UNDER FIRE

▲▲▲

An Army Chaplain's Memoir

ROGER BENIMOFF

with Eve Conant

THREE RIVERS PRESS
NEW YORK

Library of Congress Cataloging-in-Publication Data
Benimoff, Roger.
Faith under fire / Roger Benimoff and Eve Conant. — 1st ed.
1. Iraq War, 2003—Personal narratives, American. 2. United States. —Army—
Chaplains—Biography. 3. Benimoff, Roger. I. Conant, Eve. II. Title.
DS79.76.B449 2009
956.7044'37—dc22   2008050504
ISBN 978-0-307-40882-2

Printed in the United States of America

Design by Debbie Glasserman

1 3 5 7 9 10 8 6 4 2

First Paperback Edition

To my wife, Rebekah,
and my sons,
Tyler and Blaine

The story that follows is a work of memoir; it is a true story based on my materials and best recollections of my second deployment to Iraq and my return home. As a chaplain, it is of utmost importance that I safeguard the privacy of individuals whose lives have touched mine. Certain people who appear in the book gave me permission to use their actual names, and they are listed in the next paragraph. I have kept other individuals private by changing their names, identifying features, injuries, and circumstances. In some cases, composite characters have been created for the purpose of further disguising the identity of individuals.

People whose names and experiences remain un-altered include, Rebekah Benimoff, Tyler Benimoff, Blaine Benimoff, Colonel H.R. McMaster, Lieutenant-Colonel Christopher Hickey, Chaplain (Major) David C. Causey, Chaplain (Major) Ret. James Bixler, Major John Wilwerding, Captain Matthew Ryan Howell, Renee Howell, Chaplain (Captain) Geoffrey Bailey, First Lieutenant Maria Kimble, First Sergeant Wilfredo Serrano, Specialist Andrew Seng, Rose McIntyre, Jack Lederman, Specialist Brent Hendrix, and National Guard Specialist George Schmidt.

All scriptures that appear in the book are from the New International Version of the Bible. In some Psalms, the word LORD in the biblical text has been written as Lord to conform to style.

The views held in this book do not reflect the views of the Army or the Department of Defense.

C O N T E N T S

Part One **I R A Q**

1 LEFT SEAT RIDE *1*

2 GEARING UP *18*

3 CAMPING OUT *36*

4 GHOST TOWN *41*

5 CAMP CAPPUCCINO *52*

6 COLD FUSION *63*

7 COMFORT ZONE *82*

8 DRAINING THE POND *95*

9 CRASH LANDING *111*

10 48 HOURS *124*

Part Two **H O M E**

11 RUNNER'S HIGH *131*

12 WALTER REED *149*

13 SIDE EFFECTS *165*

14 TRIGGER POINTS *175*

15 HOMECOMING *195*

16 WALKING WOUNDED *221*

17 GRACE *229*

18 WOUNDED HEALER *236*

19 COMMUNION *248*

Author's Note *257*

Roger Benimoff's Acknowledgments *261*

Eve Conant's Acknowledgments *265*

Reading Group Guide *269*

We are all living in the unknown and it is a journey.
My heart is filled with prayer and
God is giving me a discerning spirit.

— ROGER BENIMOFF

FAITH UNDER FIRE

Part One

▲▲▲

I R A Q

1

▲▲▲

LEFT SEAT RIDE

I am excited and I am scared. I am on fire for God . . .
—*Army Chaplain Roger Benimoff just before start of his second deployment to Iraq*

MAYBE IT WAS just another example of how war can warp your judgment, or at least how it warped mine. But I didn't question the impossibility of leading a prayer for forty people in less than sixty seconds. Forty members of our senior command and staff had crammed into a yellow tent at our new base, Camp Sykes, a crumbling, former Iraqi airbase on the outskirts of the ancient city of Tal Afar. We were not in friendly territory.

Tucked into Iraq's most northern corner, Tal Afar was an insurgent's haven. With its dizzying labyrinth of alleyways and beehive housing blocs, the remote city was the perfect place to stockpile weapons from bordering Syria. Hidden in those alleys just 10 kilometers from us were hundreds, if not thousands, of AK-47s, rocket-propelled grenades (RPGs), improvised explosive devices, and anti-tank mines. Managing that arsenal was a growing army of technologically savvy Iraqi and foreign fighters who were, to put it mildly, displeased with our recent arrival.

First impressions always stick. I had one minute to assure these men and women, their metal chairs propped unevenly on the vinyl tent floor, that I was capable of being their spiritual and personal counselor for the next ten months. These were the people who made decisions that could spell life or death for the soldiers convoying "outside the wire" of our base and into Tal Afar. In the coming months it was likely some of these officers would be injured or killed, and we all knew it. If previous deployments were any guide, others might cave from emotional or mental stress and need to be airlifted out. There would be wives or husbands back home who would divorce them by satellite phone or e-mail. We all knew the stakes. We just didn't know who would be lucky and who wouldn't.

"Chaplain, let's begin the meeting," offered Lieutenant Colonel Harrison. He was the deputy commander of our regiment, in charge of northern operations as more than six thousand soldiers, with attached units, shifted north from Baghdad to Tal Afar to crush the growing insurgency here. This had all been so hastily put together; just two weeks earlier we were settling down close to Baghdad when suddenly we were sent up North. We hadn't trained or planned for this region, and our base wasn't yet equipped for the type of military offenses that would be asked of our soldiers in the coming months.

Nor were we prepared on the spiritual level. When operations were set up at Camp Sykes, we'd have thousands of soldiers but only four chaplains, three Protestant and one Catholic. I would be the only chaplain for my squadron of a thousand soldiers. For now, I was also the acting regimental chaplain until my superior, Chaplain David Causey, arrived in two weeks.

"Brave Rifles, Sir," I replied to Harrison. That was our motto in the Third Armored Cavalry. When approaching another cavalry soldier, you had to say "Brave Rifles," and the other had to respond with "Veterans." That dated back to 1847 when Gen. Winfield Scott, rallying the troops during the capture of Mexico City exclaimed, "Brave Rifles! Veterans! You have been baptized in fire and blood and have come out steel." Sitting there in that vinyl tent that April morning, I did not suspect that in the next ten months I would also be baptized in blood. But it would be the blood of others, and I would not come out like steel.

I did know that my tongue was dry and my palms were sweating, even if the brutally hot days when soldiers joked about the "dry" 120-degree heat were still months away. At thirty-two, I was one of the Army's youngest chaplains, but after a short break in Fort Carson, Colorado, was starting my second tour in Iraq. I should have felt experienced, instead, I was petrified. I had already started ministering to the troops at Camp Sykes—one of our soldiers had been killed near Baghdad, and one of our Bradley crews had been hit by an improvised explosive device, or IED,—but I had yet to minister to our senior command. Forty officers from the regiment and subordinate squadrons, exhausted and harried, were looking to me for a momentary escape from their personal worries and the complicated logistics of getting our squadron trained up to replace the outgoing one.

There I was with sixty seconds to give my first regimental Word of the Day. I cleared my throat and pulled a wrinkled piece of paper from my chest pocket. It was a story I had copied from a fellow chaplain, a sketch about a reporter interviewing God.

"If God granted *60 Minutes* an interview, what would he say? When asked what surprises him most about mankind, He says it's that people are in a rush to grow up and then long to be children again; that they lose their health to make money and then lose their money to restore their health. When asked what are the most important lessons of life, he says he'd like people to learn that it takes years to build trust and only a few seconds to destroy it. That a rich person is not the one who has the most but who needs the least. That it's not enough to forgive others. People must also learn to forgive themselves."

I looked up and tried to make eye contact with the men and women surrounding me. I had their attention. With only sixty seconds allotted to prayer, none of them could argue I was wasting too much of their time. I could smell the cheap plastic of our temporary shelter, momentary protection from the dry winds and organizational chaos outside. I took a deep breath and did my best to squeeze the high points of ten theology books into my remaining twenty seconds. "Many of us climb a ladder in life only to look down and discover we're on top of the wrong building. Think today about the building you are trying to scale, about what is most important to you in life. Please take a moment to do that." I now had ten extra seconds for a short prayer.

"And now let's pray. God, we ask you to watch over our regiment and to protect those who are still moving north from Baghdad. Hold us in your hands and help us keep our eyes on you. Amen."

I don't know whether I convinced the officers I was someone they could trust, but for some reason—perhaps the relief of finishing my first Word of the Day for the regimental command and staff—I felt incredibly hopeful, both for myself and for them.

There had been deaths in my first deployment—more than forty in the regiment—but the Army was learning and improving all the time. And so was I. I was learning how to counsel men and women in a war zone. These were people who were losing friends to snipers and wives to other men, often during the same week. Elation and despair. Life and death. Sixty-second prayers. A whole lifetime's worth of problems could descend on a person in the course of one deployment. In war, everything is accelerated.

The meeting in the tent went on for another hour or so, a familiar and intricate barrage of army talk on combat operations, communications, equipment status, intelligence, and personnel. When it wrapped up we all stood to salute the clearly exhausted Lieutenant Colonel and soon the tent was a churning sea of camouflage. That's when I noticed a soldier walk into the tent toward Harrison. I was about 10 feet away and couldn't hear what the soldier told him, but I saw his face flinch and then tighten. The colonel's brown eyes scanned the room, looking for someone, quickly settling on me as he issued my first order, "Chaplain, get over to your squadron right now—there might be casualties. . . ."

I don't remember what else he said because I was already running. We had only been on our base eleven days and already there were casualties? I had heard that the outgoing squadron hadn't been varying its entrances and exits to the city when they convoyed, meaning they were easier targets for insurgents. Please God, I thought, don't let this have been caused by a lack of planning, I ran 150 meters to our Tactical Operations Center. They had heard the incident might have involved a Stryker vehicle and an IED. I was moving quickly but I felt like I'd been kicked in the stomach and anvils had been tied to my feet. Somewhere a whistle blew and the race began.

▲▲▲

WHEN IT RAINS in Iraq, the sand immediately turns into mud, more like quicksand than the packed crystals you might leisurely track your footsteps through at the beach. The Army was, by now, well versed in the ways of this Iraqi mud, and as I raced toward the chapel and my parked Hummer, I had to hop my way across thousands of small rocks scattered around the base as stepping stones. I dashed under a concrete arc designed to block mortar attacks aimed at the chapel—my home, my office, and my sanctuary—before reaching my Hummer. I prayed a silent thank-you when I saw Specialist Andrew Seng, my assistant and bodyguard, standing by it with his 9-millimeter in a holster and his M16 draped over his shoulder. The aid station was on the other side of the camp in an aircraft hangar set up with tents for triage, sick call, and surgeries. It wasn't far away and we felt our camp was secure. But we had just convoyed up from a base that was mortared the day I arrived, so I took nothing for granted and it was a relief to have Seng by my side. I was in a unique position here. Even though my rank was Army captain, a pocketknife was the most lethal object I was allowed to hold. Chaplains are never allowed to carry weapons, and that's a good thing. I wasn't in Iraq to fight. But I still felt awfully vulnerable.

Even our Hummer was no guarantee of safety. Soldiers were dying in better vehicles than ours. Our Hummer was called *Headquarters 10*. It was old, its tan paint was chipped, but it was a step above the Hillbilly Armor many of our soldiers used in our first deployment. It seemed sturdy enough, and, believe me, we were thrilled to have it. *Headquarters 10* had "add-on" armor doors with steel plating more than an inch thick bolted onto each side, a new engine, and a bulletproof windshield. It was the underside that was worrisome. Seng had laid eight or nine sandbags on the Hummer floor to protect our legs from shrapnel in case we drove over an IED. We crawled up into the Hummer, with me trying to twist and contort my right leg over the sandbags to reach the gas pedal. There was no better protection under our legs because when this war began, no one in the Army had anticipated that roadside IEDs were going to become the insurgents' weapon of choice.

Eight soldiers must have been inside the Stryker, a technological feat ten times safer than our Hummer, when the explosion hit. One would think an IED would be no match for a Stryker. The eight-wheeled behemoth, with its convex-shaped hull, was designed to deflect IED blasts away from its center, where the soldiers sit. A Stryker is surrounded by what looks like a chain-link fence, so that any incoming RPGs (rocket-propelled grenades) would hit the fence and explode before impacting the vehicle.

I had a feeling the insurgent's handmade explosives had won this round of our bloody, science-fair competition. If there were any survivors, they'd be taken to the aid station first, and I wanted to be by their side. If they asked for a final prayer before death, I could do it; if they just wanted a hand to hold, then I could be there to offer mine.

The trip took less than five minutes. We drove on badly paved roads, past our gym, until I slammed on the brakes in front of the aid station. Seng and I ran out of the vehicle but quickly realized we were the only ones rushing. Several officers and noncommissioned officers (NCOs) from Grim Troop were outside the aid station, some crying, some pacing, but no one was running. That's when I knew I wouldn't be counseling any injured soldiers. I would be counseling the soldiers left behind, the ones who had just lost a member, or perhaps several members, of their family. I would say *friends* or *buddies* but those words are often too weak to describe the relationship. How often do you entrust someone with protecting your life? Usually a parent plays that role. Or, if you're elderly, perhaps an adult child. If you're a soldier, it's the people in your unit.

We soon learned that four soldiers had been killed—two from my squadron, both in their twenties, after less than two weeks on base. Pvt. Michael Simmons Jr., known to his friends as a loyal soldier, card player, and junk food connoisseur, died instantly. Pvt. First Class Edward Belmont, who had no large aspirations in the Army but still outperformed everyone else, died of severe trauma to the lower body, which is a clinical way to say that his leg was torn off. The four remaining survivors were evacuated to a larger base with better medical facilities. Two had only minor scrapes. One would have his leg amputated and suffer mild traumatic brain injuries. The other, riddled with shrapnel, would retire from the Army within months.

Word of the blast had gotten out. Next to their living quarters just beyond the aid station, the troop leaders had gathered the hundred-odd soldiers who had served with the now dead and injured. As the command and I walked over to address them, I fell into step next to our squadron commander, Lt. Col. Christopher Hickey, a family man in his early forties, with dark hair and a soft-spoken manner. We had become friends back at Fort Carson and I figured he must be thinking what I was—that this was a disturbing start to our deployment. What could we possibly say? This would be no sixty-second Word of the Day. This would be combat ministry in all its intensity.

It may sound strange, but I prayed for talent. Not for the talent of showmanship or a quick tongue, but for the ability to somehow, through some miracle of the human heart and mind, assure these soldiers that these were not meaningless deaths, that we were all part of something worth risking our lives for. I wanted them to know that God was walking with them in their grief. As I thought about what to say, their troop commander, Capt. Ryan Howell, asked them all to "Take a knee." He and First Sgt. Freddy Serrano had just identified the bodies back at the aid station and requested that soldiers from a different troop to handle the bloody cleanup of the Stryker. It would have been too much for our troopers to handle during their first days here.

Hickey spoke first: "You're probably asking yourself, why do I do this? Less than one percent of us serve the nation, and all I can say is thank God we have troopers like these two." Next he did the smart thing—encouraged these heartbroken soldiers not to retaliate against the civilians of Tal Afar. "The enemy wants you to go into town and start killing everybody but they do not know that we are a professional, disciplined force. We will not fall for that. Most of the people in that town want safe, fulfilling lives like you do. You've seen their kids, the ones that look like our kids. . . . You do not fall for the temptation to take out your anger on innocent Iraqis."

I scanned the soldiers' bloodshot eyes. Anyone who thinks soldiers don't cry hasn't been on a battlefield. Most of them were no more than twenty years old, yet they had 20/20 vision when it came to their own mortality.

It was getting dark but the temperature still hovered around 90 degrees. Soon it was my turn to talk. I told them it was okay to grieve and to cry. That they had lost two close friends and that I was there for them if they needed someone to confide in. Then I read Psalm 121, one I knew by heart, thinking it might offer some hope for the months ahead:

> I lift up my eyes to the hills—where does my help come from? My help comes from the LORD, the Maker of heaven and earth. He will not let your foot slip—he who watches over you will not slumber; indeed, he who watches over Israel will neither slumber nor sleep. The LORD watches over you—the LORD is your shade at your right hand; the sun will not harm you by day, nor the moon by night. The LORD will keep you from all harm—he will watch over your life; the LORD will watch over your coming and going both now and forevermore.

I asked them to pray with me, and all one hundred of them, kneeling in the dirt, lowered their heads. The air was filled with diesel smoke and our nostrils were dry and burning from breathing in desert air and tank fumes. I could hear helicopters flying near our base and the ever-present sound of tanks in the distance.

"God, as we grieve the loss of these soldiers, we look to you as our help, our guide. It's impossible for us, alone, to make sense of this. Please be with the families of these four. They don't know it yet but they'll need you today. Help us to heal as a troop and provide us wisdom and patience as we carry out our mission. . . . Amen."

As the gathering broke up, I went from platoon to platoon to make myself available to the soldiers. Human contact can often be more healing than words. It's best not to speak, just to be there. If someone is crying or appears to have gone numb, I will put my hand on their shoulder. Another small way to express empathy is to mimic a person's body position. If a soldier is kneeling, I will kneel; if he is sitting, I'll seat myself close by. My most important duty that day was to be a quiet presence, to let them know that I was walking, sitting, or kneeling with them in their grief.

Later that night I dropped onto my metal cot, tucked into the corner of my office at the chapel. During our convoy up here we had slept three hours over a three-day period, and we were living off of adrenaline. None of us had much time to catch up on our rest since then.

I didn't bother walking to the shower trailers. When I fell asleep, I was still in my camouflage.

Late April 2005

Already, I am repeating my pattern from my first deployment. I am doing more memorial ceremonies than preaching. What this really means is that I am having to handle and juggle a lot of grief, I don't think the deaths have set in yet.

By the end of April, the handoff between our two squadrons was in full swing. Soldiers call this transition "Right Seat Ride, Left Seat Ride," and I was still in the right-hand passenger seat, taking instructions from members of the outgoing squadron on what to expect in Tal Afar. The most important lesson of all, however, was an unspoken one. It went against all the advice in psychology books but it worked. The rule: Don't let the grief sink in or you will sink with it. I had conducted memorial ceremonies for ten soldiers during my first deployment. But since then the situation in Iraq had only gotten worse. I was less than three weeks into my second deployment and the body count was already half the number I'd handled in my entire first tour. Grief would distract me from my job. So I made a decision, as I had the last time I served in Iraq, to focus on the emotions of my soldiers, not my own. The decision was mostly a subconscious one; somehow my mind knew that compartmentalizing my own grief would help me to survive. I knew there might be emotional consequences, but I was confident I could handle them. Most important was my ability to be a calming presence for the incoming troops, who were being welcomed not with a parade but with a funeral.

The soldiers were already feeling raw. Soon after the Stryker incident, I held a debriefing session with an army nurse to counsel the survivors of the attack. The Army puts a great emphasis on these Critical Incident Stress Debriefings as part of mental-health care for troops, and our job was to take the soldiers through several phases designed to help them process traumatic events.

Space was tight on the base, so this first debriefing was held in the small wooden chapel where I worked and slept. More than a dozen survivors of the convoy filed in, propping their guns at their feet as they took their seats in a circle of folding chairs. I was nervous. I hadn't led a debriefing since my first deployment and these soldiers appeared to be in a state of shock. They were supposed to be safe in those armored vehicles, yet for those just beginning their time here, it was dawning on them that in Iraq there are no guarantees; the height of American technology could easily be undone by a makeshift bomb. They had only just started their tour, the timing was unnerving, and I'm sure most of them didn't want to be in this session. They probably just wanted to crawl into their cots and turn off their troubled minds.

Each soldier recounted what he had seen. "There were tires and chunks of the Stryker flying at least fifty feet in the air," recalled one private. "How the hell could that happen?" Another soldier, his uniform and hair disheveled, kept repeating that he'd never forget all the smoke. That's a common reaction, to fixate on one image and have it loop endlessly through the mind; I knew from training to keep an eye out for that. As they spoke, I formed my own mental image of the accident: the Stryker coming apart in pieces, bodies draped over chunks of smoking metal. Those who had been right behind the Stryker appeared the most traumatized. One soldier couldn't get over the fact that he was a few lucky seconds away from his own death. But then he immediately hung his head in shame, as if he'd been celebrating his own survival at another's expense. It's called survivor's guilt; rationality goes out the window when you see the people right next to you—people you care about—torn to pieces.

The assurance of God's presence at such an awful moment is a hard idea to embrace and this was not an appropriate time to talk about scripture or faith. This was the time for soldiers to explore their own feelings, and I was relieved to see some soldiers crying. The ones who worried me were those who didn't talk. They sat there glassy eyed or stared at the floor. When it was their turn to share, they lowered the heads and muttered, "I'll pass." There were long moments when the only sound was the chapel's undersized air conditioner struggling against the rising temperatures outside. I made a mental point to check up later on the quiet ones.

At ten on an early May morning, we held a memorial service for the fallen soldiers. As I stood in the shade of a hastily built stage, I couldn't help but be overwhelmed by the immensity of the moment. There must have been 850 soldiers in attendance. Many had attempted to "press" their desert camouflage for the occasion. The uniforms always came out of the dryer wrinkled, which didn't usually matter. But for a memorial service, soldiers tried to get their hands on small travel irons if they could.

There was classical music playing from the loudspeakers as everyone gathered. "Lord, please allow my words to honor you," I whispered to myself as I stood up and approached the podium. I asked the crowd to stand for the national anthem and then led a short prayer

asking God to "remind us of your presence, that as
we mourn their loss you will be our strength and our assurance that you have prepared a place for all who love
you." I took a breath and began a meditation for the
four. These men embodied army values, I explained—
including loyalty, selfless service, integrity, and personal
courage. They gave their lives for another. As Jesus says
in the book of John, "Greater love has no one than this,
that he lay down his life for his friends" (15:12–14). I
looked out at the soldiers and told them of a time in King
David's life when he cried "I am worn out from sobbing.
Every night, tears drench my bed; my pillow is wet from
weeping. My vision is blurred by grief; my eyes are worn
out because of all my enemies." My voice was hoarse but
I spoke as clearly as I could about how grief can so easily
turn to anger and helplessness. "Our call is to take our
pain, which is very real, and honor the fallen with a new
sense of purpose, by carrying out the values that they
gave their lives for."

After ten minutes at the podium, I sat down while the
troop commanders addressed the hundreds of soldiers
kneeling or standing in the heat. Many of them, like me,
were wearing their cavalry Stetson hats and spurs, cavalry
honorifics earned from previous deployments to Iraq. At
that moment in time, I felt like a member of devoted,
close-knit community, and I was deeply proud to be part
of this family.

But I also noticed that many of the soldiers were
stone faced, like uniformed statues in the sand. Most of
them were just starting a one-year deployment. A good

number were still teenagers. They were thousands of miles from home in the most dangerous country on earth and most of them didn't even own a passport, since the Army doesn't require one. Maybe they enlisted because of 9/11. Maybe they just wanted a fresh start in life or desperately needed money for college. The needs were all different, but the effect of the attack was the same: Any notion of immortality they might have harbored was already being chipped away. Most people don't start thinking about death until they're walking with a cane. But here in this crowd of teenagers and twentysomethings, the thought of death was about to become a constant companion.

2

▲▲▲

GEARING UP

Early May 2005
I know this is a meaningful and instrumental time in my
life, being involved and impacting people for God. I am
thankful to be in the position where God has placed me and
hopefully one day I will look back and see His work. But
there are a lot of people who are grieving and they need God.

I WAS LESS than three weeks into my deployment and
five young men were dead. It was almost too much to ab-
sorb, and it wasn't until after the memorial service for the
Stryker soldiers that I had a moment to be alone in my
office.

I had yet to call Camp Sykes home, but I already
knew my first furious weeks here would shape my
thoughts for years to come. I knew it would be important
to have a spiritual base—for myself and for my soldiers—
but my office and bedroom in the chapel were a mess. All

five of my 100-pound heavy-duty black storage trunks
and several of the boxes I brought with me were wedged
against the walls; the rest of my chaplain gear was still sitting in the Hummer outside or in a cargo container due
any day now. I sat down on a duffle bag so giant I could
have slept in it. I was exhausted and overwhelmed, and I
hadn't even unpacked yet.

I felt deluged and knew the soldiers felt worse. They
were the ones on the front lines, but I knew from my first
deployment that it wasn't always easy to reach them. The
Army wanted chaplains, psychiatrists, and all mental-
health teams to have access to the troops, many of whom
were marooned in outposts scattered throughout Iraq.
But half of the time there wasn't enough space in the convoys for us. If soldiers were suffering, they'd have to ask
the chain-of-command to send help, and if you know soldiers, you know that won't happen. Yet how could I argue
my way out of the chapel and "outside the wire"—beyond the perimeter of our base—if I couldn't even keep
my eyes open?

I'd just have to do better. I promised myself no soldier
under my care would ever have to ask, "So . . . who's our
chaplain again?"

Feeling overwhelmed was par for the course, in no
small part because the U.S. Army had a shortage of chaplains. In all branches of the military there were about
2,700 chaplains ministering to an active-duty force of 1.4
million. That equaled about 1 chaplain for every 518 service members. The Army had about 1,200 chaplains and
each of us oversaw anywhere from 500 to 1,000 soldiers.

In peacetime, when we chaplains could focus on marriage or adjustment issues, those ratios were adequate. But with wars in Afghanistan and Iraq growing more violent by the day, soldiers needed intensive counseling, and a lot more of it. It was hard for the Army to recruit chaplains; not only were repeat or extended deployments the norm, but requirements were strict: Chaplains must meet all the requirements to become a commissioned officer, pass fitness tests, go through a chaplain officer basic course (a sort of chaplain boot camp), have a bachelor's degree and a seminary degree in theology, and be endorsed by a recognized denominational group. Many chaplains are also trained in suicide prevention, marriage and family counseling, and grief counseling. Last but not least, we must be willing to work in a war zone and willing to do it without a gun.

Most chaplains I knew did their best not to let it show if they were scared. But we were in places like Iraq without weapons and I, for one, counted that as rather scary. We took precautions and we carried our faith as our defense, as an invisible shield that we prayed would protect us and radiate out to envelop our soldiers. At times that felt like an emotional mission impossible; other times it felt like the simplest, most straightforward thing—walking alongside soldiers and helping them through their spiritual struggles.

The word *chaplain* comes from *cappa*, the Latin word for "cloak." According to legend, a pagan Roman soldier named Martin of Tours saw a freezing beggar and cut his cloak in half to share it with the man. After dreaming of Christ dressed in the same cloak, he converted to Christianity, devoted his life to the church, and was later canonized a patron saint of France and of soldiers. Martin's portion of the cloak became a holy relic that soldiers carried into battle for protection. The *cappellani* were the priests who guarded the sacred half-cloak; eventually all priests associated with the military became *capellani* or now, in English, "chaplains."

During the Civil War, chaplains would comfort the sick and wounded and even serve as postmasters, writing letters for injured and dying soldiers, many of whom were illiterate. In World Wars I and II, they ministered and gave final prayers, collected the dead, and conducted burials. Chaplains died alongside soldiers in the field and, as in the case of the Korean War, languished in POW camps.

According to Pearl Harbor lore, "Praise the Lord and Pass the Ammunition" was a chaplain's calling cry. But we are trained as chaplains that pushing soldiers to fight is a commander's role, not ours.

Vietnam, with all its moral ambiguities, presented new challenges to the chaplaincy. Some chaplains supported the war publicly, and after the Mỹ Lai Massacre, many Americans who opposed the war questioned whether chaplains were providing a religious mandate for an indefensible war. The lessons of Vietnam were examined by all in the military, including the chaplaincy. During my chaplain basic course, we studied the massacre as part of an ethics lesson on how to recognize bad decisions and confront the leaders who make them. If a chaplain learns of an order that seems illegal or immoral, or violates Geneva Conventions, it is the chaplain's duty to lodge a formal complaint and take all action possible to raise attention to the problem.

Chaplains are of all faiths; there are Catholic, Jewish and Muslim chaplains in the military. But the majority of chaplains like me—a Baptist—fall under the generalized category of Protestant. We are not allowed to evangelize soldiers toward any particular faith; those of us who try are reprimanded. U.S. law also provides for the free practice of religion for all soldiers, which strictly prohibits any insensitive action that would prevent a soldier from practicing his or her beliefs. For example, on Jewish holidays, Jewish soldiers have the right to be flown in a Blackhawk to a base where a minyan (the number of persons required by Jewish law to hold a religious ceremony, usually at least ten) can be successfully gathered. At the same time, the combat mission always comes first; there are no allowances made for Christmas, Easter, Sabbath, or anything else if combat is underway.

Soldiers come from all belief systems, from Islam and evangelical Christianity to atheism. In Iraq, I've seen many wearing crosses; some carry pocket-size, camouflage New Testaments, its index listing topics such as Fear, Loneliness, and Duty. Some huddle in prayer before they go on patrol, others find God for the first time while serving on the battlefield. U.S. soldiers have been baptized in the Tigris River and atheists crossing the Iraqi sands in their tanks have converted on the spot after reading, *"Even thought I walk through the valley of the shadow of death, I fear no evil."* The opposite can also happen. Some lose faith that God, or whichever higher being they worship, can provide safety in the desert of Iraq. I know of at least one soldier who committed suicide at his base's chapel. Life and faith are always accelerated when death is close at hand.

A soldier's religion or lack of one didn't change my duty to each one. I was in Iraq to counsel anyone who asked for it, to walk with a person through his or her ordeal. Providing what is known as a "ministry of presence" simply meant I was there for a soldier if he or she needed a companion, a willing pair of ears to listen to their sacred stories.

It is an honor to walk with soldiers of all faiths, and I am happiest when serving others. But early in my ministry I was uneasy about just being a presence. I thought it was important to always be *doing* something. It took a while for me to understand that just being a good listener, being a calm, secure anchor in the midst of chaos was actually profoundly helpful. I try to maintain a discerning spirit so I can be attuned to the needs of others by sensing their nonverbal cues, by understanding the environment the soldiers and I are placed in, and by maintaining my own bond with God.

I could walk a soldier through his troubles, but chaplains are not psychiatrists, and we are not qualified to diagnose or treat major disorders. There are military psychiatrists, psychologists, and clinical social workers trained as mental-health caregivers. That said, spirituality and mental health, for many believers, go hand in hand.

They say that God can be found or lost in a foxhole.

What I knew from my first deployment was that war rarely leaves a person's faith untouched. Many soldiers asked me versions of the same basic question: How can you reconcile a God of love with a God who allows the terror of conflict? What makes a war a "just" war? "Thou Shalt not Kill" is a phrase we've all heard at some point in our lives, but under certain conditions why is it somehow acceptable for armies to slaughter one another? There's a way to wriggle out a technical, lawyerly answer to that, but the soldiers who asked that question were concerned about how it applied to their personal actions. It was hard to come up with a satisfactory answer for them.

War is unjust yet we find myriad ways to justify it. My theology has been that we are made in God's image, but our actions can often be flawed. We elevate ourselves above God by making decisions about ourselves and others without God's direction. Pride becomes the motivator not only for individuals but for nations. Nations decide to fight for their security, values, beliefs, and ideologies, often invoking God as an excuse, and its citizens kill accordingly. In World War II, multiple nations waged war against fascism. We justified our position: in order to save lives, we had to kill others.

Before becoming a chaplain I did not have doubts about war being a just response to unjust actions. It was only after two deployments that I started to evaluate my beliefs more closely. I did not want to get involved in the politics of the U.S. intervention. I wanted to do what most chaplains have traditionally done in war—minister to the needs of soldiers. So I put complex questions about the nature of war in what I called my mystery cup—the collection of mysteries I wished to solve but couldn't yet comprehend—and tried instead to focus on the specific spiritual and emotional issues my soldiers presented me with.

Ministering may sound morally rigid to some, or like a black-and-white pursuit, but in practice it is more like diving headfirst into a murky pool of moral quandaries. Soldiers' personal lives didn't stop just because they were fighting in a desert; in fact, the distance often aggravated problems at home. Broken communication, buried fears, and emerging questions about the nature of their existence all combined to make Iraq a military, mental, and spiritual battlefield. I wanted to pray with my soldiers, walk them through scripture, and help keep those who believed on their path to God or whatever their personal anchor was. But ministry takes many forms. Like most things in life, it didn't quite turn out as I had planned.

▲▲▲

I NEVER THOUGHT I'd become a pastor or a chaplain. I thought I'd become a cop or a detective, somehow involved in criminal justice. Maybe I had watched too many action movies, but it seemed I'd always been attracted to the idea of a right and a wrong, of rewarding the just and catching the bad guys.

I was born in 1972 to parents of Jewish ancestry, who divorced when I was six months old. My mother and stepfather moved our family from Jackson, New Jersey,

to Austin, Texas, when I was seven. I didn't see my bio-
logical father much after that, but my mother—who had
become a Baptist—was always with me, and she would
tell me that God would use me in a special way.

As an eight-year-old I walked the aisle to accept
Christ because my older sister Bonnie had, and I looked
up to her. By my junior year of high school, I wanted a
more genuine relationship with God. But I lacked a clear
understanding of what that meant. I already had authority figures in my life, and like most teenagers, didn't take
too well to being told what to do. But I had the idea that
if I trusted in God, everything would somehow turn out
okay, that I would be better for his guidance.

At nineteen and at a loss over what to do with myself,
my stepfather, Gary, suggested I join the Army. It had
helped him find purpose, and he thought it could do the
same for me. I knew I needed discipline, and, at the very
least, enlisting would give me time to sort out my future.
I became a private and a fuel specialist, which meant I
drove tankers, delivering fuel to the mechanized infantry.
Army life meant drinking and partying with my buddies,
but active duty also taught me how to set a goal and
achieve it. I learned I could be tougher and more successful than I'd ever imagined. This would be key for me later
in life: I'd pursue something and through sheer persever-
ance, drilled into my head from boot camp, I would get
it. In a way the self-confidence became addictive.

By the time I finally made it to college I sensed a
deeper calling from God than I'd ever felt before. I joined
the First Baptist Church in San Marcos, Texas, and not

just because one of its members, sophomore Rebekah McIntyre, was so gorgeous. I first met her in the pews but then came across her again at a Hawaiian-themed welcome event at the Baptist Student Union. Her devotion to God ran deep, and I wanted the same for myself. That desire was given a boost when the pastor of our church took me under his wing. He was the exact opposite of what I had grown up with, the "hell, fire, and brimstone" pastors who used God as a boogeyman to make me behave. He taught me that what was important was my *relationship* with God. For the first time in my life I was meeting people who didn't see God only as an authority figure; they also saw him as a friend. I had never considered that possibility, and I clung to the idea that I was now able to develop a personal relationship with God, a being that suddenly seemed to have as much interest in my life as I had in His.

During my sophomore year, I started to ask myself some real questions: What can I do in life that will have meaning? I had spent time earning a paycheck and that was not enough. What can I do that might have an eternal impact? I sensed a call to devote my life to God, but I could think of one hundred reasons why I wasn't fit to be one of God's servants: I was not a public speaker, I was an introvert, and I wasn't exactly the brightest person in any given room. But with each disqualifying remark, I somehow felt that God wanted me and accepted me as I was, an imperfect creation dependent on Him. The "Moses pericope" in Exodus convinced me that God would provide what I needed to carry out my newfound calling in life: Moses was just God's vessel; his shortcomings didn't matter. Somehow that helped me believe that things would work out for the best if I relied on and deepened my faith.

With that decision my life began to fill with love. I married that beautiful sophomore Rebekah, and after completing my Criminal Justice degree, I enrolled in seminary. During my second semester, our son Tyler was born. Blaine was born two years later, shortly after I had begun my residency as a hospital chaplain.

Throughout my studies, I remained in the National Guard, at first as a fuel specialist and then as a chaplain candidate. I was drawn to the military chaplaincy because I thought it would be a way to serve God and my country at the same time. I felt God had given me a special affinity for soldiers, having been one myself for so many years. By the summer of 2000, I had completed my Chaplain Officer Basic Course and felt I was on my way to a life that would balance spirituality and service and family. Then came 9/11. Like many Americans at the time, I was practically shaking with equal parts determination and fear when I heard George W. Bush address the nation a few days afterward. He turned to the television cameras and said, "And those in the military, GET READY." Democrat or Republican, none of that mattered, I just went to my garage and started packing my military gear; I had a new mission.

I volunteered with the Texas Army National Guard as a chaplain for Operation Noble Eagle II, a defense mission to protect sensitive sites, like nuclear power plants. After that, I decided to reenter the Army on full-time, active duty and on July 16, 2003, I became an Army chaplain with the rank of captain.

Three weeks later I found myself assigned to Support Squadron, Third Armored Cavalry Regiment, in Al Anbar Province—the heart of Iraq's Sunni Triangle. My soldiers supplied and equipped the entire regiment; they weren't supposed to be in the trenches. But there were no front lines, so what did names like *Support Squadron* really mean? There were deaths and sniper attacks and helicopter crashes and memorial ceremonies and soldiers sent home with injuries that would fundamentally alter their lives. I learned that being a chaplain involved everything from counseling men as their marriages fell apart to identifying dead bodies. I was pushed to what I thought were my limits, but I never questioned God's steadfast presence during that first tour in Iraq. He was there for me in all ways.

Three months after I came home, I was told they were sending us back for another year.

I wanted to serve but didn't want to leave my family again so soon. Still, Bekah and I knew this was what we had signed up for when I joined the Army, so we started to prepare right away. She'd soon go back to being what we called a "geographically single mother" and, to keep my image alive in the boys' minds, she turned on our video recorder and kept it running for months. She filmed me teaching Tyler and Blaine how to do Army physical training in our living room. I wore my Army exercise gear and tried to teach Tyler to do jumping jacks, while Blaine ran around in his diaper with his favorite blanket in tow. We both nearly died laughing over Tyler's version of push-ups, which amounted to him alternately lying flat on his belly and then sticking his tush in the air.

Every Sunday we attended a small chapel on the post called Veterans Chapel. We started each service with praise songs. Then Bekah, or whichever Sunday school teacher was on duty that week, would take all the children to a smaller room for a Bible story and arts and crafts. Tyler had recently been diagnosed with type-1 juvenile diabetes, so Bekah divided her time between checking his blood sugar, teaching the kids, and singing on stage with the praise team.

We tried to pack in all we could as a family. One day I herded everyone into the minivan for an impromptu visit to the local fire station. Bekah grabbed the special backpack we kept on standby—Tyler's diabetes supplies and Blaine's Pull-Ups—and we rolled out of our driveway. Bekah didn't take Tyler anywhere without his pump, a glucometer, insulin, syringes, and plenty of "fast sugar" and protein options in case his blood-glucose levels dropped too low. When I told the firefighters I was being redeployed, they buckled us into their truck for a private tour. Bekah shot more video. Like many military families, we never said it out loud, but she wanted videos of me in case something terrible happened in Iraq.

I prepared as a father and husband and I also prepared professionally. I was still unnerved by the deaths in my first deployment, but that didn't stop me from making my upcoming deployment, which would begin in seven months, even more challenging. I asked to deploy with a Third Armored Cavalry combat maneuver squadron, Second Squadron—the kind of soldiers who drive tanks and kick down doors—because I thought they'd need counseling more than anyone. But I was perhaps also guilty of a boyish fascination with them. Being a combat soldier in Iraq seemed like the ultimate soldiering experience. If I wanted to be a well-seasoned Army chaplain, I told myself, how could I not be drawn to the toughest work imaginable?

When the chaplain assistant assigned to me, Specialist Seng, first came to my office, I was impressed. He was twenty-two, a Presbyterian, and the son of a sugar beet and cattle farmer who later became a minister. Seng had thought of becoming a pastor but when an army recruiter came to his Nebraska home and told him about the job of a chaplain assistant, he knew he had found his life's calling.

He seemed devout, and I joked with him that it didn't really matter to me what he worshipped, if anything. In a chaplain assistant I needed a dedicated soldier and an expert shooter in case we got into scrapes—an expert shooter means fewer people get seriously hurt, not the opposite. I also wanted someone good with directions, since I am a disaster with them. Seng grew up driving a tractor on a 1,000-acre farm, so even though he was just out of his teens, he was perfect for the job. He was also madly in love with his new wife, a part-time accounting student and waitress. I liked that we both had spouses we were devoted to as it would keep us both stable. He seemed guileless and in the months that followed, we worked well together. He would often complain of my

perfectionism, but always with humor. I would also discover that he was deeply loyal.

As we readied ourselves to depart, Seng worked
around the clock submitting gear requests, toiling over
the computer, and printing out worship songbooks
(among approximately 10,001 other tasks). I was working
on a religious support program for soldiers' emotional
and spiritual needs and getting trained in ways to treat
the early signs of post-traumatic stress disorder. The
Army was trying to stem the tide of soldiers coming with
PTSD in any way it could; at my request my commanders sent me to Coatesville, Pennsylvania, to learn more
about trauma therapy.

I trained my mind and trained my body. I think I did
a million push-ups to combat my Starbucks Belly. (Beer
wasn't my weakness; indulging in white-chocolate mo-
chas and desserts was.) I was getting dangerously close to
the maximum army standard weight of 174 for my 5-foot
7-inch frame, and I didn't want to be known as "the fat
chaplain." So every day Seng and I worked out with a different troop, which usually involved a 5-mile run and an
infinite amount of pushups and sit-ups.

Counseling soldiers anxious about being redeployed
was another important part of my preparations. One of
them, Pvt. First Class Brady Westin, came to me that
summer. He was 23 and with his blonde hair and blue
eyes he looked like a poster-boy for the Army. His uniform fit perfectly on his 6-foot frame. Everything about
him was in tip-top shape, except his mind. He hadn't
been formally diagnosed with PTSD but he sure showed

symptoms. When we met in my office he was subdued as he described his first deployment: guarding gravesites, shooting an Iraqi insurgent who was about to shoot him, winning a prestigious army medal for successfully defending his squad members from enemy fire. He struggled with the concept of killing another person—even though he had seen the enemy's eyes and it was either kill or be killed. Brady wasn't religious and we only talked about his work and emotional life—the little he seemed capable of holding onto lately. He wasn't married and was in a long-distance relationship that was drying up. Like most people exhibiting signs of PTSD, he had trouble with intimacy.

I was worried about Brady as was my mentor, Chaplain James Bixler. We counseled him about once a week, but little seemed to help. When I worked out with his troop, I'd keep an eye out for him, but he was always standoffish. Perhaps he was embarrassed about the counseling. Later that fall he flew out west to try to mend ties with his girlfriend. They broke up. Even if he wasn't capable of showing any deep emotions at that time, I could tell in counseling sessions that he was devastated.

In the months before we deployed again, I learned that Brady had married a different woman. He no longer sought therapy, so we weren't sure how he was doing or if he had overcome his PTSD. This happened often; the pace and mobility of military life meant I wasn't always able to follow up with soldiers as I would have liked.

Our departure was imminent, and Iraq seemed to be growing more dangerous and deadly by the day. It took only simple arithmetic to calculate there would be more casualties in my second deployment than there had been in my first. I asked myself, what I could do better this time around? I couldn't prevent the deaths, but at the very least I could help the survivors process those deaths in a healthy way. I decided it would be a good idea to formalize a Standard Operating Procedure for memorial ceremonies. I went to work developing a CD that included all the music, paperwork, and organizational steps required when a soldier is killed. It sounds grim, but in a war zone having a blueprint for memorializing death is a positive thing. It allows soldiers and commanders to focus on helping each other and processing their grief, not paperwork.

I wrote a memo detailing the order of a ceremony: national anthem, invocation, tributes, meditation by a chaplain, "Amazing Grace" played on the bagpipes, last roll call, firing of volleys, and then "Taps." The soldier's flag-draped casket would have already been rushed home a few days earlier, but sometimes the soldier's boots, gun, and helmet would remain with us during the ceremony to honor him. The manual also stipulated that a Critical Incident Stress Debriefing should take place before the memorial service. Chaplains who had special training, like I had, could volunteer to help with the debriefings, which assisted the survivors in processing their thoughts and feelings within 24 to 72 hours of an event. The Fort Carson chaplain's office sent me to the basic and advanced courses to become certified. I would be leading dozens of these sessions in the coming months.

I also included various documents I hoped would reduce the amount of administrative stress that comes with the death of a soldier, including a sample condolence letter, materials on grief counseling, and file recordings of the national anthem, "Taps," and "Amazing Grace."

These were the nitty-gritty details of death. I hoped our regiment wouldn't have to use them when we deployed again. But somehow I knew this unfortunate blueprint would come in handy.

3

▲▲▲

CAMPING OUT

Early May
It seems no matter how close to God I draw, there is always
a part of me that is incomplete.

IT WAS EARLY May 2005, just over a month into our deployment, and we were already low on personal supplies.
Our Forward Operating Base, or FOB, was more like an
outpost than the well-equipped superbases in Baghdad
and Mosul and we were practically camping. Everyone
was running out of shampoo, soap, deodorant, and ra-
zors. These were creature comforts, and it meant a lot to
the troops to have them. But for days I hadn't been able
to e-mail or call friends back home to beg for shipments
because of the communications blackout due to the four
soldiers recently killed. This was standard procedure;
whenever there was a death in our area, our Internet and
satellite phones would be turned off to make sure that the

family members would get notice through official chan-
nels, not word of mouth.

I lived out of two duffel bags. One held gear including seven sand-colored T-shirts, seven pairs of under-
wear, my eye-droplets (I had laser eye surgery before
redeploying; glasses were a real handicap to me last deployment), a laptop, and my $70 REI inflatable sleeping
mat. I had also learned from my last tour that this mat
was indispensable, especially since I would sleep on the
ground or in cots when I visited troopers in the city. The
other bag was stuffed with CDs like Bibleworks 4.0 and
sermon illustrations for the projector, an army combat
helmet, and a Kevlar armored vest, bulletproofed to a
level capable to blocking 7.62X39mm bullets, the typical
discharge of AK-47s.

Seng's duffel bags had been loaded down with a supply of three M9 magazines and six M16 magazines. He
also carried a M16A2 rifle and a military-issue Beretta
92F 9-millimeter pistol with him at all times. In Kuwait
Seng had been issued the rest of his ammo, which he
stuffed into his load-bearing equipment—a suspender-
type, desert-colored ammunition belt with pouches.

He was equipped with ammunition—which I prayed
he'd never have to use—and I was equipped with DVDs.
I had stocked up on titles I knew would be in demand: "So
You're Getting Married," "Before You Say 'I Do,'" and
"Master Your Money Workbook." I also brought 129
children's books (for soldiers to read to their kids over the
phone), and relationship books like *His Needs, Her Needs,
Fighting for Your Marriage, Surviving an Affair,* and *Torn*

Asunder. Those last two dealt with extramarital affairs, a big problem for soldiers. And I always kept a good supply of communion wafers and cups, guitar strings, checkerboards, and easels.

There were two other items I kept with me at all times. One was a small brown leather Bible that Rebekah's aunt Laura and uncle TJ had given me as a gift. The Bible fit perfectly in my chaplain's kit, which I strapped to my body armor any time I traveled to conduct services. The other was the result of a successful eBay bid, admittedly one of life's greatest little thrills. For sixteen dollars I bought what should have cost sixty—a Crane's full-grain, leather maroon journal with thick white pages and gold trim edges. I had never attempted to keep a journal before. When it came in the mail to our home at Fort Carson, it struck me as so fancy I hoped my writing would do it justice. I never imagined I'd confide in it through the entire deployment and the year after I returned home.

My first entry was written back in January in Colorado.

This journal contains my thoughts and feelings as I approach my second deployment to Iraq. We have been working seven days a week, there is so much to do and there is little time to do it. Sometimes I take a step back and look where I am at and it is hard to believe that I am a combat veteran. I cannot lie; serving in a combat environment, going into harm's way, and putting my life on the line makes my adrenalin pump. Something happens when your life is put in

danger and worldviews shift. I once thought that I was in-
vincible. I thought I would live forever. But I know that isn't
so. Flying on helicopters after one has just been shot down.
Going on convoys after an ambush attack makes for a sober-
ing reality. Returning after serving 7 months & 18 days
and receiving the welcome I did makes me proud to do what
I do. But more than that, coming back with the people I
served with and having the memories we do is just as mean-
ingful. My call to ministry and the meaningfulness of serv-
ing in the Army brings fullness to my life.

It sounds so rosy as I read it now. Only three days
later, as my journal and I were getting to know each other
better, the hard truth started to creep out:

Late January 2005, 37 days until the deployment
It's been a pretty tough day today. I think the catalyst was
seeing Chaplain Diggs. He just returned from Iraq. Talk-
ing with him took me back to my unresolved feelings. He
shared a story of a woman who God put in his path and then
she was killed in action. As the day approaches, I am experi-
encing the reality and the heaviness of the deployment. I
don't know if I can take it. My heart cries out and I have an
awful feeling when I think about Iraq. "Dread" is a more
appropriate word to describe how I feel about the fatigue I
know I will walk through. I know I need God and this can-
not be done w/out Him. He is my hope, strength, and focus.

Now, several weeks into our time in Tal Afar, I kept
my Bible and journal with me at all times. I also had a

support group. Before deploying, I had asked several of my friends and mentors from previous units to be available by e-mail. I believed in prayer and I knew this group would be my lifeline. Even if their prayers were channeled through the mysterious pipeline of silicon chips and satellites and twisted wires to my computer at 2:00 a.m. Iraqi time, they felt as real, timely, and momentous as the dozens of armored vehicles just beyond my chapel windows.

4

▲▲▲

GHOST TOWN

Mid-May 2005
It's about 45 minutes until my Saturday night worship ser-
vice begins and I am relaxing a bit. It has been a busy day. I
counseled four soldiers, went to meetings, and coordinated
for our new chapel. I am really enjoying my work and seeing
a new "greatest generation" develop. Our soldiers are very
brave and are of the highest caliber of men. I am also get-
ting to impact soldiers spiritually and personally as they go
through this difficult time. It is satisfying and I thank the
Lord for putting me in this position. There are so many peo-
ple back home who want to help and can't. I am in the mid-
dle of history! I miss Rebekah, Tyler, and Blaine and I know
that the Lord is working in their lives.

As I SETTLED into my new home for the next eleven
months, military and security websites were describing
our camp as one of the most dangerous in Iraq.

We had all heard the news of the successful U.S. storming of Fallujah in 2004. But the truth was that many of Fallujah's fighters simply fled north to Tal Afar. Only 40 miles from the Syrian border, the city was a key staging point for trafficking men and weapons toward insurgency hot spots like Mosul and Baghdad. We were camping out just a few miles from a massive safe house for some of Iraq's most violent insurgents.

By the middle of May, about four thousand soldiers had arrived and were stationed at the camp. There was one troop from my second squadron already outside the wire—Heavy Company. The others—Headquarters and Headquarters Troop, the 43rd Engineers, Eagle, Fox and Grim Troops, and Lion Battery—were still at the camp. But we all knew it was a matter of time before most of them would have to move into the city and take back Tal Afar from the insurgents. Previous efforts had been half-baked. Six months earlier some 800 U.S. soldiers working with Iraqi forces had launched an offensive on the city, giving its 400,000 inhabitants a much-needed semblance of order. But then they withdrew, and by October the insurgents had come back in force and regained control. The locals were feeling scared, abandoned, and angry. Most of the police force had disbanded and sided with the insurgents while religious leaders and school-teachers had been replaced with followers of radical Islamic sects. We were told that the city's hospitals and doctors were allowed to care only for fighters. Shops were shuttered. Burned cars littered the streets. If anyone in the civilian population opposed the insurgents or, worse, helped our troops, one of three things happened:

They were kidnapped, shot, or beheaded; their bodies were often left on the street as examples. The city felt like a death trap, a ghost town run by insurgents who were ever present but never seen.

My first time traveling outside the wire was in late May when I rode into Tal Afar with the command and their security detail, a dozen soldiers in three Bradley Fighting Vehicles. (Up here it was too dangerous to roll the streets in anything less than a tank.) There was no room for my assistant, Seng, in the Bradley and I needed to get to Heavy Company for a Sunday service, so I decided to brave the city without him.

The plan for the day was twofold. Our first destination was the Tal Afar General Hospital. Two weeks earlier Fox Troop soldiers had recaptured the hospital, running off insurgents who had turned it into a triage unit for their fighters. Now a platoon of about thirty U.S. soldiers was guarding it around the clock. I would check in on how the soldiers were faring while our squadron commander Hickey met with Iraqi politicians also visiting the hospital. Then we planned to convoy to Fort Tal Afar, an old Iraqi prison that was now a training post for the Iraqi Army, where I would conduct a service for the one hundred Heavy Company soldiers stationed there. I hadn't counseled with any of Heavy Company since they had set up at the fort two weeks earlier and was worried some of the soldiers might be feeling out on a limb.

The stakes were always higher outside the wire. Tal Afar was not safe, and I knew from my first deployment that being away from the main camp was tough. Soldiers lacked the small comforts of the base, like omelettes made to order or the retail therapy of our little store, where you could buy DVDs, cookies, and peanut butter. Instead they ate cold scrambled eggs and stale biscuits for breakfast, often wore the same dusty and sweaty uniform days in row, and slept with little AC in summer and minimal heating in winter. Living outside the wire also meant soldiers were constantly in danger and had fewer private moments to share their concerns with friends or superiors, let alone a chaplain. Since they couldn't come to me, it was my duty to go them.

When we drove up to the hospital, it was clear that conditions were rough. The building resembled an army fort more than a safe haven for those in need of medical care. Two Iraqi soldiers in full body armor holding AK-47s ushered us past the concrete dividers that blocked the entrance to the building, and two more Iraqis guarded what appeared to be the exit. Looking up I noticed that the perimeter of the hospital's roof was lined with sandbags 4 feet high, broken in two places where Iraqi soldiers had bunkered into makeshift machine-gun nests—nooks where small holes between double-stacked, dusty green sandbags served as openings for the barrels of their weapons. The exterior brick walls of the hospital were the same faded, sand-drab color as the rest of the city's façade, except for where fresh bullet holes left gaping marks in the brick.

Inside the hospital there was none of the buzzing activity of a typical emergency room; the dead quiet was broken only by the occasional murmured conversations of Iraqi doctors and soldiers. Few civilians seemed to think it was safe to come here. Maybe they knew something we didn't. Everyone and everything seemed to be drifting quietly toward the center corridor of the hospital. That's where the doctors conversed and where soldiers had lined their cots so that when they slept, they'd have a few walls of cushioning between them and the snipers.

I felt like I was in a time warp. The black-and-white floor tiles reminded me of hospitals I'd visited as a kid back in the seventies, but the equipment was even older—it looked like something from the 1930s. I felt the curling finger of depression tug at my chest. How many of Tal Afar's sick and injured were hiding in their homes or in some makeshift refugee accommodations, with no access to even this level of care? No one seemed to be keeping track and I wondered if we'd ever know the real number of Iraqi casualties. The anonymity of the suffering was hard to accept and it didn't help that there was little I could or was supposed to do about it. We had taken back the hospital from the insurgents, and now townspeople who risked their lives to come here were treated with some of the most archaic medical equipment I had ever seen.

I rested on a large windowsill on the first floor of the hospital's exterior corridor and tried to clear my mind. During our ride I had been deep inside the Bradley's hatch and seen nothing of our journey. I wanted some sense of control, some perspective on where we were, but the hospital window was pockmarked with sand and blurred with dirt accumulated from months of neglect. A feeling of control was a rare luxury in Iraq, and I realized it was fruitless to try to capture it.

I heard footsteps. Moments later three Iraqi doctors walked past me in their white lab coats, whispering to one another in Arabic—were they friend or foe? Doctors were starting to treat the few civilians who made the dangerous trip to the hospital and we were pleased with that development. But we'd also been warned by informants that several of them were complicit with the enemy. The doctors spent all day cooped up in the hospital with our soldiers and we had no idea if some of them might still be loyal to the insurgents. All my life I had lived in awe of doctors; suddenly I feared for my life.

I noticed an Iraqi man and a little boy enter the hospital and walk toward the window where I was perched. The boy had a makeshift cast on his arm and wore a girl's Gore-tex jacket that had probably been passed across the world as a global hand-me-down. It had faded to a dusty, peach color and the sleeves hung below his arms. The boy wrapped himself around his father's leg and looked up at me. To him I must have looked like all the other soldiers. I wore camouflage, a helmet, and a bulletproof vest. He probably didn't notice that instead of an M16, two fountain pens were tucked into the loops on my body armor or that above my name patch was a small brown cross. Instead of ammunition, my vest was equipped with the two chaplain's kits I always carried with me. One contained my Bible, Daily Bread booklet, and a small ringed binder with operation orders and worship materials. The second held all the accoutrements for communion: wafers in a pill-box–style plastic container, a metal cross, a metal chalice, a camouflaged green shoal decorated with small black crosses stitched at the bottom that I draped over my shoulders and chest for services, small cans of grape juice, scraps of paper with Words of the Day, a flashlight, and a military issue strobe light for signaling MEDEVAC (medical evacuation) helicopters.

I tried to think of what I could pull out of my kit to entertain him. He stared at me as if I was from Mars, yet his eyes were warm and curious. I couldn't help thinking about Tyler, now five, and Blaine, just two. I smiled, put my hands over my eyes, and started to play peek-a-boo. The boy giggled and covered his eyes. We took turns, both laughing. His father noticed our game and broke into a smile.

That's when it dawned on me that I was being careless. What was I doing sitting in front of a window? I quickly moved farther down the corridor closer to the boy. We played a bit more peek-a-boo and eventually I pantomimed good-bye, since the only Arabic I knew was *Inshallah* or "If God wills it," which didn't quite fit the occasion. I headed up to the hospital's second floor to join our sergeant major who was headed up to roof, which was being guarded by Fox Troop and Iraqi soldiers. We walked up another staircase and opened a door. The sunlight was blinding. Even after I put on my sunglasses, my eyes felt like they were on fire.

Four Iraqi soldiers in two machine-gun nests sat manning their positions while six U.S. soldiers were milling about the dusty, concrete roof—one cleaning his M-16 rifle, a few talking with one another, one or two walking the perimeter, looking down over the sand-bags lining the roof to the streets below. From here you could see almost the entire city of Tal Afar, which spanned out below us in a palette of two colors: pale sandy brown and cement gray. The sprawl of two- and three-story buildings was interrupted only by the minarets of several mosques. Five times a day the loud-speakers perched inside those minarets heralded the muezzin's call to prayer.

In some ways I had begun to fear that sound. I admired the Muslim people for having specific period of prayer set aside each day, where all their worldly tasks took a second seat to their faith. I also knew that for many the Islamic faith was a path to spiritual peace. Back at Fort Carson I had been happy to assist a Muslim soldier who was trying to meet the faith requirements of Ramadan. But here in Tal Afar, as a soldier and a chaplain, I couldn't help but fret when I heard the sound. Insurgents stored munitions in mosques and it was hard to trust anyone, whether they were people of faith or not. There had been some discussion at camp about whether some of us chaplains should meet with local Imams, but the idea quickly faded. Frankly, I was relieved. I wanted my mission to be limited to my soldiers, not expanded to local politics, especially in a place and at a time when religion was so inflammatory.

With my body armor on the roof felt even hotter than the 90 degrees it was outside. But if I was a bit disappointed to be up on this roof at high noon, it wasn't because of the heat. Forget Hawaii—northern Iraq had the most beautiful sunsets I'd ever seen. Five hours later the sun would blaze a fiery red and the drab buildings, usually indistinguishable from one another, would come alive in bright pink. But now, in the midday sun, the light was flat and blinding, which—a moment later—made it very hard to tell where the bullets were coming from.

Out there in the glare was a sniper, or maybe several. In an instant, machine-gun fire erupted all around me.

Adrenaline coursed through my body. I'd never been shot at before and everyone else on the roof had a weapon but me. Unarmed and out of my league, I jumped behind a metal intake duct as the Iraqi soldiers emptied their machine guns into what seemed like every nearby building. Our soldiers, crouched behind the sandbags, were scanning for targets. I realized that even with my helmet and body armor, my back was totally exposed. I hunched my shoulders, hoping that my helmet and flak jacket, crunched together, would somehow protect the bare skin on the back of my neck that always got sunburned. I heard a few more single shots fired in our direction and, somewhere in the distance, a crashing metallic sound like a giant metal hubcab wobbling in place and then falling. Why had I gone outside the wire without Seng? Moments like these were the whole reason the chaplain assistant job *existed* and I had hopped in the

Bradley this morning without him. My gamble had not paid off.

Forty seconds passed with no gunfire, so I ran across the roof to where the six Fox Troop soldiers were now positioned. The eldest must have been in his midtwenties, the youngest eighteen. I crouched between Specialist Tyson, who had an M16A2, and another sergeant, who also had a M16 in hand and a 12-gauge shotgun strapped around his back. I must admit, it felt much safer to be close to those guns.

Tyson swiveled his gaze away from his gun and gave me a smile. "I've never seen a chaplain-in-action . . . pretty cool." Very funny. I laughed, but inside I was petrified.

We crouched and waited—three minutes and no bullets. Everyone stood up, so I did too. Why was Iraq so surreal? We had just been someone's target range and now we were standing around like nothing had happened. I tried to look cool and collected, not in a rush, no sir, of course not, as I made my way to the door leading back inside. Just before I reached it, an Iraqi soldier accidentally pulled the trigger on his AK-47 and a deafening shot rang out. My entire body jerked in fear and I felt on the verge of throwing up my own heart. He had shot a hole through the rooftop, not 2 feet away from me. He said something sheepish in Arabic and laughed. If these are the good guys, I thought, we're in trouble. I said a quick prayer that God protect all of us and dashed inside.

As we convoyed out, the radio chatter inside my Bradley was focused on finding the sniper's location and, needless to say, my Sunday service was not exactly being hotly discussed. Two Apache helicopters flew in as backup while we searched, but after an hour, we hadn't found a soul. We gave up and returned to camp.

5

▲▲▲

CAMP CAPPUCCINO

Mid May
The Army must be warping me because it was not a big deal
to get shot at. It didn't seem real.

A FEW DAYS later I closed the door to my chapel office, sat down at my desk, and reached for my greatest solace in secular life, my coffee grinder. I was blessed: my Uncle Jack sent me small shipments of Starbucks from the United States. In the still desert air the smell of the freshly ground beans was pure magnificence. I turned on some classical music using an iPod hooked up to computer speakers and brewed a few cups in case someone came in. I hoped they didn't, though. The adrenaline of my trip outside the wire had worn off and what I really needed was time alone.

I had done scores of counselings in just the past month and several soldiers from other squadrons had started to come to me. Maybe it was the Starbucks or the fact that there were not enough counselors to go around. But I hoped it was in part because I tried to be a good listener.

Within a month or so we'd have four thousand troops positioned in the area and only four chaplains on the base. I didn't know it yet, but for much of the deployment we'd also have no psychiatrists for our troops and only one clinical social worker. There would be marriages and psyches falling apart and not enough health-care workers to try to patch them together.

The frequent counseling improved some of my skills while it chipped away at others. I often focused more on the soldiers in front of me than on God. Because I had a strong clinical background, it was often possible to depend on my clinical skills, not my faith or God for guidance and confidence.

For many of us, this was our second deployment, and if it might have taken a year to get worn down before, now it could happen in months. Even though it was still early in our tour, the skill I feared losing most of all was what counselors call "differentiation": the ability to distinguish someone else's problems from your own.

Differentiating is important for the survival of the counselor and for the patient's progress. Without it, the counselor might start focusing on his own thoughts and emotions and then project or "countertransfer" them on to the person he is counseling. If a soldier is confiding in me about family problems, it's important that I don't assume she's dealing with the same problems I am—like distance from my parents or my fear that after two deployments, my young sons were forgetting me. But as a professional, I couldn't bring into the conversation any disappointment or anxiety about my situation—it wouldn't help the soldier and it wouldn't help me.

Already, I knew I was regressing a bit. It was hard not to associate with the soldiers' anxiety and exhaustion: We wore the same uniforms, ate the same meals, and each night we laid down to sleep with many of the same fears. A staff sergeant had recently rapped on the door of my office at the backside of the chapel. I had just finished designing my office for privacy, blocking out my windows with an American flag and a piece of cardboard so people wouldn't see who I was counseling. The sergeant was shaking and as soon as I let him in, he started to cry. I motioned for him to sit down on my dilapidated brown couch, at that time the only couch on the base, a luxury even if its pinstripes were faded with stains and its cushions were so worn there were holes in them.

The staff sergeant told me his wife was cheating on him but that it was his fault. He had been too tough on her, too insensitive, and now she was moving on. If he could go home, he might somehow stop the divorce proceedings, but the Army doesn't make allowances for that. He was brokenhearted with disappointment, mostly in himself. My mind flashed to Bekah for a moment—I was thankful she was devoted to me, but I knew my long absences were hard on her, especially with Tyler's diabetes. Maybe I ought to call her today, I thought. But I needed to focus on the sergeant; the most important thing was to help *him* identify his feelings and thoughts. I put my own fears aside and we talked for over an hour about how he might cope.

As more soldiers appeared at my door with more stories, I was like a glass already full, but someone kept pouring more water into me anyway. Fatigue was settling into my body for the long haul, like a houseguest with no departure plans. Perhaps I was hoping that when you love your work and trust God as I did, the glass itself gets bigger.

Late May 2005

We lost another soldier last night. Master Sergeant Albright was killed-in-action from an RPG [rocket-propelled grenade] at the Tal Afar hospital. What a loss . . . LTC Hickey, while talking to Yellow Platoon, said it in disgust— "He was guarding a hospital." I just feel so down. Last night it was hard for me to feel at all. Today, I feel tired and depressed. We had a ramp ceremony last night and saw Albright off. The hardest part of this is seeing my troopers suffer. It is like a heavy load is on me and I wish I had Rebekah to help comfort me. I do need to pull to the Lord during this time. I need to involve the Holy Spirit in all aspects of my life. My prayer is that I would seek the Lord with all of my heart, with all of my mind, and with all that I am.

Albright was killed at the same hospital where I had been shot at just a few weeks earlier. It hit home that any of us could die at any moment, and that reality was numbing. When I first heard the news, I walked over to the aid station where they brought his remains in order to be present for anyone who needed it. I walked around the aid station and spent time with small groups of soldiers from his troop, many of them in tears. No one talked much, we just stuck together.

After the death of Albright, we held a Critical Incident Stress Debriefing for his troop. This was the first of many that I would perform with First Lt. Maria Kimble, a licensed clinical social worker and combat stress debriefer attached to our regiment. She was Italian, small and serious, with dark brown hair and black-rimmed eyeglasses, and she knew how to put people at ease. For most of our deployment she was the only behavioral health officer for our base and for all of the soldiers scattered in and around Tal Afar.

We had pulled the twenty soldiers who witnessed Albright's death away from their duty at the hospital and expected them at the chapel any minute. Seng had set up chairs in a small circle and was already at the door. During the session, it was Seng's job to guard the entrance of the building so that no one would interrupt the discussion. Soon the soldiers, dusty and tired, filed in past Seng and they slid into their chairs.

I scanned the room, making eye contact with the soldiers. We all knew each other but I followed protocol with a formal introduction. "Hello, my name is Chaplain Benimoff, and . . ." I motioned to Maria.

". . . my name is Maria Kimble." In the course of the deployment, we would become great partners in situations like this. Where I was boisterous, Maria was calm.

She was thirty-three and teased me about being my senior—by a whole seven months. I liked working with her because she seemed to take soldiers' needs to heart. She liked working with me because she said a person would never know I was a chaplain unless they wanted religious guidance, that I didn't walk around blessing the troops and instead presented myself like just another soldier.

I started the meeting by trying to establish a sense of direction for our talk. "Good morning, we're here today to process our thoughts and feelings about Master Sergeant Albright. You guys have been through a lot and I just want to give some ground rules before we start. I ask that you speak just for yourself and not on behalf of anyone else, to respect differing viewpoints. I also ask that you stay in this circle until we finish. Lieutenant Kimble and I are here to facilitate. Any comments or questions?"

Silence and the shifting of chairs.

"Okay, thank you. First I want to go around the circle and ask you to recount the facts as you know them in regard to the attack against Albright at the hospital. Please share your name, your role in the event, and the facts as you saw them. Let's start here." I motioned to the soldier sitting to my right who looked about nineteen. He kept his eyes to the plywood floor but took a slow breath and started to whisper.

"Our section had some downtime. A bunch of us were playing cards with him." The soldier paused. "Then he got up to go to the bathroom across the hall. That's when we heard it."

He looked up and locked eyes with me. "We jumped up and ran to the hall," he said, swallowing something caught in his throat. "He was lying there with his head split wide open. His brain and his blood were all over the walls, on the floor."

The soldier looked up at the ceiling, paused, and then continued. "Just a minute before, we were all laughing and joking. Then he was gone, like it happened in an instant." Another soldier reached over and patted his back, making that hollow, timeless sound I've heard so often in Iraq that sums up so much of what can't be put into words.

We went around the circle. I could picture the scene all too vividly. The discolored floor tiles, the Iraqi doctors we didn't know if we could trust. A rush of fear and dread washed over me but I pushed it away.

"If only he had waited to go to the bathroom," one of the cavalry scouts was telling Maria. "I woke up and knew something bad was going to happen," said another. "I should've stopped him from going back into the hospital. We were outside earlier and he was talking me down because I was getting really upset with this deployment. He was on my track with me." Being "on a track" with someone means traveling with them in the same nonwheeled vehicle, such as a tank.

The soldier explained that the two had convoyed together in Tal Afar earlier that day. Ten minutes after Albright walked into the hospital, he was dead. When he heard the explosion, he raced into the hospital just as two Iraqi soldiers were running in the opposite direction, down the stairs, one of them stopping to vomit.

At the other end of the circle a soldier was crying silently. Another was bawling outright and got up to walk around the chapel by himself for several minutes.

It wasn't unusual for soldiers to feel responsible for the deaths of their friends. This same group had been on the hospital roof with me when the sniper attacked us. One of them was Specialist Tyson, the one who had joked with me about being a "chaplain-in-action" after I dove away from the sniper's bullets. This time he wasn't smiling or composed. In fact, he had no expression at all. Back on the roof that day he had been able to take control of the situation, while I ducked for cover and cowered in fear. But Albright's death seemed so fast and so random. There was no way to defend him. Their friend had stood up to go to the bathroom in the middle of a card game. Now he was gone. What a waste of life.

These guys trained together, joked around together, slept in the same room. In time, and for a time, they knew their buddies better than they knew their families. I know from my thousand or so counselings with soldiers over the past two years that losing a buddy is not the same as losing a friend. It's like being a big brother and not grabbing your little brother's hand fast enough before he slips off a bridge. He looks up at you in wonder and disbelief as he falls to his death. Soldiers are supposed to protect each other. When they fail, the guilt can be debilitating.

Soon, Albright's wife and children would be notified. My mind flashed to a moment between deployments, back at Fort Carson, when I was the chaplain on duty for a death notification. I was one of those people ringing the doorbell, the kind of person the family doesn't want to let in. I remember standing outside the home in my full dress Class A uniform. It was hot that day. We had parked on the other side of the street so we wouldn't give away our presence prematurely. The notification officer with me, the one who would deliver the actual news to the family, was doing this for the first time and was terribly nervous. He was about the same age as the dead soldier. A woman let us in, opening the cheap wooden door as if it was made of lead. She was standing near her stairs when he officially told her, and that's when she collapsed in our arms.

Years before I had worked in a level 1 trauma center in Dallas, Texas. On numerous occasions I stood with the doctors as they gave the bad news to loved ones after stabbings, shootings, or car accidents. But that time with the notification officer was different—the dead young man wore the same uniform I did. I had spent the last ten years either in seminary, training as a pastor, or training as a chaplain, but there was no way I could be a calming presence to that woman. I remained on the floor with her, eventually shifting her body to help her sit on the stairs. I believe I helped her in her grief as best as any chaplain can in that type of situation. I tried to reassure myself I was doing God's work, even if the most I could do was catch her fall. Any moment now, halfway across the globe, Albright's mother would be getting the same news after a knock on the door by another officer and chaplain.

Maria and I sat with the soldiers for another hour, taking turns through each phase of the debriefing. I asked them the first question: "What do you remember?" She asked the second question: "Can you please tell us what went through your mind during the event?" I asked the third: "What was the worst part for you?" She asked the fourth: "What part still causes you pain?" Then I asked the fifth: "Have you experienced any changes in behavior, physical state, or outlook?" As the soldiers spoke, I looked at them in the eye, wishing I had a giant pair of wings to wrap around them or to fly them out of this horrible place. Instead, before sending them back to their work, I went over the "teaching portion" of our debriefing; which included a rundown of the warning signs of PTSD. I also made it a point to encourage the soldiers and let them know I was honored to serve with them.

"I want to thank each of you for sharing. Each of your stories is holy and sacred. As you can see, you're not alone in your feelings. Listen to each other, console each other," I urged them. "If, about a month from now, you're not able to sleep or are losing appetite, or if you keep replaying a sort of internal tape of these events, then that is a red flag to get some help," I said, adding that they could come to First Lieutenant Kimble or me. "Our minds were not designed to witness the traumas of war, and overbearing, intense memories can seem to get locked into our brains. This is a *normal* reaction to an *abnormal* event. I just want to say that I'm serving alongside the bravest and next greatest generation. I'm proud of you guys. God Bless."

At Albright's memorial ceremony I led a meditation from Psalm 13 that I hoped might address some of the fears of the soldiers. "'How much longer do I have to suffer?' asks the psalmist. 'How long must I wrestle with my thoughts and every day have sorrow in my heart, how long will my enemy triumph over me?'" A direct answer is never proffered, I explained. "Yet the psalmist comes to say that he trusts in God's unfailing love. How is that? It's because the personal threat of death is countered by a memory of past trust and in anticipation of future deliverance." It's faith.

I urged them to remember what God had given them in the past and to trust in that future. "When we look at our call to duty, we are often placed in a position where we are stretched; we are taken out of our comfort zone and as a result, we can lose heart and become fearful. This is the time when we take to heart what Gen. George Patton stated: 'Courage is fear holding on a minute longer.'"

I folded up my notes. A bit later, a staff sergeant delivered a shorter speech. He said a soldier had come to him and asked, "Why would God take such a good man?" and how, to be honest, he didn't have an answer to that question.

None of us did.

6

▲▲▲

COLD FUSION

Early June 2005

I got to talk to Bekah on the phone this morning using Chaplain Causey's cell phone. It was so nice to not have to wait in line but it was even better to hear her voice. I have not been able to call her for a week due to the suicide in support squadron and the death in longknife squadron. I am so in love with her and I want everything to stay this way.

I have also enjoyed going through The Purpose Driven Life *by Rick Warren. It has great truths in it and has been feeding my spirit. It is reinforcing what spiritual maturity is about—complete obedience to God. I am getting a more realistic picture of who I am—a sinner who tries to control people and time. I am often frustrated at my inability to do either. If I could release my perceived control to God, then I would be more trusting toward God and my relations with others would improve. I am truly fighting an intense warfare against my self-centered nature. Rick War-*

ren states that if we will completely surrender to God, we will experience God's peace. I have experienced this and nothing compares to it, yet I struggle to surrender. God please help me, I don't have the answers but I know you do. Help my life, every aspect, every encounter to be worship toward you.

FOR MORE THAN a month, all of our soldiers in and around Tal Afar had been in full swing trying to rid the city of insurgents. But most operations lasted a few hours before the soldiers came back to camp, a strategy our command would later admit was flawed. The other day there had been a breakthrough: The cavalry learned from an informant the location of more than thirty high-value targets in the troubled Sarai district of town and were plotting a three-day offensive. Our second squadron had been in at least two sustained firefights with insurgents and lost two men in Sarai, an ancient and inaccessible district with narrow alleys that our vehicles couldn't access. The terrain would make a large operation all the more complicated and dangerous.

I asked to go out with the soldiers, as close to the front lines as possible, but during a briefing realized there would be no room for my assistant, Seng. I couldn't go without him and I was distraught. Six hundred troops from my squadron would be involved in the battle and I wanted to be there for them.

The command was tense during the preoffensive briefing. When the meeting concluded I quickly tucked my journal in my pocket and stood up to talk to my squadron executive officer, Maj. John Wilwerding. I had a problem, but he soon made it clear that he didn't need any more problems that day.

"Sir," I said, "I see that I can't take my vehicle or my assistant for the mission, which basically means I can't go."

"That's right, Chaplain."

"Sir, I'm with the soldiers 24/7, so why should I stand back now?"

"Because you will be a bullet magnet and I see no point. You can do last rites, I understand that, but there's no time for counseling out there."

He also didn't want to displace two fighting soldiers to make room for me and Seng.

But if most of my soldiers were out on a mission, I didn't want to lose credibility with them by not taking part. I wanted to be in the field with them and I needed my own vehicle to do my best job. But to Wilwedring, I was an "asset that had to be managed." I was the only chaplain for the nine hundred soldiers under his watch and he couldn't afford to lose me.

"If you go down, I've got no one to cover for you. It's final. This conversation is over."

"Sir, a chaplain from Support Squadron could cover for me if anything were to happen. I need to go and I need to bring my assistant for protection."

Wilwerding looked at me as if he were speaking to a five-year-old who needed sentences repeated.

"Chaplain, I said NO!"

"Sir, I'm going to have to go to Lieutenant Colonel Hickey on this one," threatening to go over his head.

"Get outside NOW!"

This wasn't good.

I figured he didn't want to have this discussion in front of the other officers, so I made my way outside the bunker into the harsh, late-morning sun. The major followed. We walked across an ancient asphalt driveway to a single, spindly desert tree about 10 meters from the bunker.

I stood at parade rest, my hands crossed behind my back as a sign of respect, as the major started to yell. "When I say no, I mean NO! I don't care if you are a chaplain. You are not being professional. . . ." He started cursing for several minutes without any letup. I asked for permission to speak but he refused. By that point several of my fellow officers were watching us. The major finally got so mad he just walked away.

I was shaking with anger. I was most upset that he called me unprofessional. Maybe my expectations were unrealistic given our resources, but my request was a legitimate one for a chaplain to make, and he should have respected that.

Wilwerding and I had something of a love-hate relationship, and in quieter moments our conversations often revolved around our differing views on God. We enjoyed sparring, and neither of us would ever give an inch.

"I have a lot of use for God," he'd tell me, "but not for religion." He had grown up Catholic and attended a monastic university, but would not attend my sermons, or anyone else's.

"You can always pray all by yourself then," I'd suggest.

"No. If God is a forgiving God, he will forgive me for not praying."

"God will forgive you, and wants a relationship with you."

"Religion is a concept of man," he'd continue. "Man is flawed, so religion is flawed. The reason we're here in the first place is because of religion."

"Sir, I am praying for you."

Wilwerding would get annoyed but realize I wouldn't give up, it was too much fun to harrass him.

"Keep at it, Chaplain."

"Yes, Sir."

But this time he was dead serious. He was not going to budge and allow me on the front lines, so I'd have to think of an alternative. A few hours later I inquired about going to the Forward Aid Station, FAS, with the medics and got clearance for that, but again was told I couldn't bring Seng with me. I didn't want to take that risk, nor did Seng—he was still angry with me for getting shot at on the hospital roof.

That night, still bent out of shape after being yelled at, I wrote in my journal, *I am working through a forgiveness prayer regarding Major W., and it is quite a challenge.*

▲▲▲

THE OFFENSIVE—OPERATION Cold Fusion—started two days later. To my surprise, I was told Seng could ride with me to the FAS and that we'd have our own armored Hummer for the mission. God was watching over me. Wilwerding probably also realized I wasn't going to leave him or his superiors alone until I was allowed to play some role in the mission. I woke up the next morning at 4:00 a.m. to join the convoy that would set up our aid station about 10 kilometers south of Tal Afar. We were due to depart within the hour.

It was still dark when I grabbed a toothbrush and a liter of water and stepped out of my hooch, my sleeping quarters in my office at the back of the chapel. There was no running water supply on the base, it was ferried in on tanker trucks. Brushing outside was quicker than walking the 250 meters to the shower trailers, so I walked a few feet toward the concertina wire that surrounded the chapel and our bunkers, poured the bottled water onto my toothbrush, and brushed my teeth in the dark.

After loading my chaplain gear into our Hummer, I drove to the convoy staging area and waited for Seng. It wouldn't take long to drive to the aid station but the easy distance didn't mean it was a safe trip. I realized this would be the first time I had driven in what we called blackout conditions since my fuel specialist training days back at Fort Riley. Some of the soldiers were busy putting infrared CHEM-lights on their vehicle antennas while others did their final vehicle maintenance and service checks. I prayed for no last-minute technical failures and asked one of the soldiers for two CHEM-lights to mark the front and rear of our Hummer. The infrared lights would only be visible to someone wearing night-vision goggles, not to the plain eye. That way our guys could see me but the insurgents could not.

I had butterflies in my stomach, but I was excited to

be part of the offensive. I had spent my life training for one mission or another. Now there would be no report cards and no margin for error. I made a note of the time. It was 4:30 and where was Seng? We were about to leave and my assistant was nowhere to be found.

I pulled off my body armor and made my way to Seng's quarters. He had been prepping us until late the night before and was still fast asleep. I shook him awake and told him he had five minutes. Moments later he raced out and we all boarded our vehicles. The diesel fumes filled the air as Seng and I flipped on our night-vision goggles. We were both irritable. He had been roused suddenly from a deep sleep and I was annoyed that we nearly missed the convoy I fought so hard to get us on. We barely spoke.

We rumbled through the dark for about thirty minutes and arrived at our new Forward Aid Station as the sun was coming up. We parked tactically, facing away from the FAS site in case a speedy exit was necessary. Then the soldiers fanned out to create a security ring while the medical teams determined a triage site. The officers set up what we called a command track for radio communications between our command elements and the soldiers carrying out the offensive in the city. Our aid station was starting to take shape.

A clutch of medical vehicles was parked in a square with a large, sand-colored canvas net strung over the center area. The medics were busy unloading their triage stretchers and medical equipment while 30 meters away, half a dozen of our cooks had been pressed into labor setting up for detainee operations. That meant creating a holding cell, which in this case was a circular patch of dirt ringed with concertina wire. There were about fifty of us trying to quickly transform the barren desert into an aid station and prison. I helped the medics set up a tarp to shade the triage site and checked on people in the different vehicles just to see how they were doing. I paced the perimeter of our makeshift aid station, praying for all of us inside the invisible circle that enveloped our troops and the innocent civilians of Tal Afar.

Our aid station was completely exposed and we had limited gunpower. There was one army doctor with a pediatric specialty at the station and more than a dozen combat medics on hand. They could do their best to stabilize a soldier before evacuation to the nearest field hospital in Mosul; our trucks and barren ground, we understood, wouldn't be enough to provide serious medical help.

By 7:30 a.m. it was already 100 degrees, and I was drenched in sweat as I walked around in my 25 pounds of gear. I sat down on the ramp of an armored vehicle where I could overhear the radio chatter coming from inside it. Our troops were taking the insurgents by surprise and everything seemed to be going well. That's when, in the distance, I heard what sounded like a huge blast.

A plume of black smoke rose over a corner of the city, which I gathered must have been the neighborhood in question. Fifty-caliber machine-gun fire erupted, stopped, and started up again. I looked up and saw two Kiowa Warrior OH-58D helicopters rounding the city. One of the helicopters to my right was spewing white smoke and made an emergency landing. The radio traffic was at fever pitch. Moments later there was another blast, more gunfire, and then black smoke rising from what I thought might have been a huge IED. Through the radio chatter I heard a distinct word—MEDEVAC—which wasn't a good sign. A soldier had been wounded in an ambush. The medics quickly double- and triple-checked their oxygen tanks and equipment and prepared to pounce on the Fox Troop Medical armored personnel carrier as soon it arrived.

The Medical Track came tearing up five minutes later. I stepped back as four medics gathered to unload and carry the wounded soldier to the triage station. But when the vehicle's ramp lowered, the crew inside looked grim. Despite the efforts of one exhausted medic who continued to administer CPR, the man was dead and they were delivering a corpse.

The soldier's uniform was already cut away, standard procedure in order to inspect and triage him. A medic and I started searching through his gear for an ID. I had seen gunshot victims before in my hospital days, but nothing like this. There must have been at least seven bullet holes through his torso and neck, with multiple bullet holes in his legs. If you could condense months of a deep depression into a flash of total despair, that's what it felt like at that moment to look down at his vandalized body. A medic fetched a black, multi-ply body bag. He unzipped it on top of a new stretcher and the medics silently hoisted the dead soldier on top of it.

I went back to searching through his gear, laying on the ground next to his body and finally found a laminated white "weapons card" (a weapons card was issued to each soldier to match armor to their weapons), which listed him as Maj. Brendan Shaw.

The medics dispersed to catch their breath. We didn't yet know that Shaw was a husband and a father, a skilled craftsman and a teacher. We only knew that we were all in this terrible race together, and he wouldn't make it to the finish.

After ten minutes had passed, I invited the medics to join me in a small semicircle in the shade of an armored personnel carrier to pray for him. About half said yes— the others were either uncomfortable with prayer or simply needed more time alone. Seng also hung back; he had seen Shaw's body and appeared to be in a state of shock. I let him keep to himself and turned to the distressed medics. Praying with medics was something I always offered, no matter whether a soldier had been stabilized or had died. Shaw's body lay on a stretcher on the ground, and we joined hands and circled him. Over the din of rumbling engines and radio chatter I read from Psalm 37:1 of David, "Be still before the LORD and wait patiently for him; do not fret when men succeed in their ways, when they carry out their wicked schemes."

We bowed our heads.

"Lord, our God, as we are gathered here, we lift up Major Shaw's family. In the coming days, they will learn of his death. Our words fail us here but you, Father, know our hearts. So we ask for your Holy Spirit to intercede on our behalf. Lord, I also want you to lift up the medics. There was little they could do and I ask that your peace would be with them in this time of loss. We pray these things in your name. . . . Amen."

Later that day I stole a moment to write in my journal.

I didn't know Shaw but seeing his body and thinking about his family back home made me so sad. Is the pain and heartache worth it? I don't want some medic putting me in a body bag. I found myself seriously questioning what I do. We are only three months into this and I am starting to question my purpose here. With each passing day my strength and fortitude weaken. It is like a workout in which I am pushing myself to continue and I know even if I keep pushing myself, I will fail. I have never failed professionally and the thought of such is too much to bear. God please let me look to you and no other; this is an opportunity for me to find strength through you and only you.

I felt as helpless as the medics did. We were all care-givers; we had strategized, prepped, traveled, and set up that Forward Aid Station in order to help soldiers. Instead we were useless, the power and bloodiness of the events surrounding us had easily overtaken our hopeful aims.

For the next two days we waited in the heat as our soldiers continued to fight in town, thankful that no one else was brought to us.

▲▲▲

ABOUT THREE DAYS after Shaw's death I drove in my Hummer to the Military Transition Team's location on the other side of Camp Sykes. These were the guys who had served with Shaw. This was an especially important debriefing session because these soldiers were National Guardsmen who had drilled together for years. Back at home their wives were in the same mommy groups; the families barbecued with one another on weekends while the kids ran underfoot. When I asked them now about their emotions—"What is the worst part for you?" and "What part of this sticks with you?"—several started to cry. When Shaw was killed, the soldiers lost not just an officer, but a leader of their community.

Losing Shaw heightened the soldiers' worries over their own safety, and our session expanded into a discussion of their fears about being in Iraq. Being a part of the Military Transition Team meant they trained and served alongside Iraqi Army recruits, an arrangement that could often prove fatal, as it had in the case of Shaw, who had been patrolling alongside Iraqis. Insurgents made it a special point to target the new Iraqi Army soldiers, who often lacked the expertise or level-headedness to accurately fire back. Our soldiers also felt they were too understaffed and overworked to effect any real change in the Iraqi Army. When I ended that debriefing, I felt proud to have worked with such dedicated soldiers and I hoped I had made some small difference in their stress levels. But with so much of their work still ahead of them,

I could feel the heavy weight of unfinished business on my shoulders.

The memorial service was the next day. The Iraqi Army soldiers who trained with his troop were invited, and I had written and collected prayers that I felt would honor Shaw, who was devout Christian. The bulletins had been printed and included Psalm 91, which we called the Soldier's Psalm, and which his commander had wanted. It began with "He who dwells in the shelter of the Most High will rest in the shadow of the Almighty."

Twenty minutes before the ceremony, an order came that conflicted with our plans: One of our regimental leaders cornered me and Chaplain Causey in the mess hall and told us there would be no scripture reading; he requested we be sensitive to the Iraqis present and hold a ceremony free from any religious overtones. I interrupted him and told him that we were not going to change what we had already prepared, and that this would have to be resolved by his superiors. If a soldier was Muslim or Jewish, we would have held a ceremony that was suitable for their tradition. Yes, we needed to show respect for the Iraqi Army, but in death what mattered was the belief system of the victim; *that's* what we needed to honor, not politics.

After much debate, Chaplain Causey led a meditation and gave the invocation and benediction. The bulletin remained unchanged and so did the Christian nature of my prayer, "Give us strength to go forward from this day, trusting, where we do not understand, that your love never ends. Bestow upon us the understanding to know you, the diligence to seek you, the wisdom to find you, and a faithfulness that may finally embrace you. We say good-bye to a devoted soldier and we thank you for the impact that his life had on us. Give us now your word of hope, that may look to tomorrow, to see hope beyond grief. It is in your name that we pray, Amen."

Mid-June 2005
Just got done counseling a soldier who is broken up. His wife told him that she wants a divorce. There is little he can do to fix the situation and he made a passing comment that he was going to hurt himself in order to get home. Times like this make me appreciate the wife I have and the Lord who has protected me from making stupid decisions. There were many opportunities to mess things up and God has watched over me. Thank you Lord! I am quite lonely these days but God continues to keep me on track, on focus.

Counseling was in high demand. Each month I had to send in paperwork about all my activities; by June it was clear that Seng and I were pushing our limits. Looking at the numbers on my report, I wondered how any of us—chaplains, soldiers, medics—were able to do so much with so little. That month I held six Protestant worship services for 73 soldiers and conducted 42 counseling sessions, most dealing with stress or marriage issues, 3 dealing with grief. I visited 436 soldiers and assisted with one memorial ceremony. I conducted 23 Word of the Day devotionals with a total attendance of 895 soldiers and held 8 critical stress debriefings for 94 soldiers. I also conducted 5 reunion briefings, which soldiers going on home leave had to attend. I would prepare them for what might happen—their homes might look different or their children not recognize them—and say that they shouldn't rush in like bears and start taking things over, but should take it slowly. I also held suicide prevention briefings for 62 soldiers, held 5 Bible Studies for 26 soldiers, and helped 9 soldiers record DVDs for their families.

I tried to keep myself centered by focusing on prayer and meditation and seeking God's counsel. On off-hours a group of about five soldiers and I would go through Rick Warren's *The Purpose Driven Life*, which covers forty days' worth of devotionals. Each one emphasized a different spiritual topic that focused on our purpose for being on this earth. That simple message helped me refocus and remind me why I was in Iraq, to assist soldiers but also to grow as a person and pastor. This was a spiritual testing ground, and following God was reserved not only for the times of joy but also for the times of sorrow. There was a verse I read often before deploying, Philippians 4:11b–13:

> [F]or I have learned to be content whatever the circumstances. I know what it is to be in need, and I know what it is to have plenty. I have learned the secret of being content in any and every situation, whether well fed or hungry, whether living in plenty or in want. I can do everything through him who gives me strength.

In a way this was my motto. The secret of being content meant trusting that Christ would provide for my actual needs over the course of the train-up, the deployment itself, and the return. This is what I tried to instill in my soldiers on a daily basis. "Being content in any and every situation" means traveling in a hostile environment for days on end, facing endless grief tied to human loss, enduring the everyday reality of death, lacking sleep on a consistent basis, being hungry, being cold in the winter and hot in the summer, and yet still having an inner connectedness with God.

When I accepted God's call, I was not free to name the conditions I would be facing. In my case the calling was two deployments to a hostile combat theater. When push came to shove, though, I did have needs. I wanted a consistent God with whom I could commune every day, one who would give me strength to endure the heartache of Iraq.

We couldn't see the end in sight, but those of us who were believers truly did wish to "do all things through Christ." As we studied *The Purpose Driven Life*, I realized I was trying too hard to control my situation and the people around me. I needed to give up that need for control, including my need to control my relationship with God, in order to be spiritually mature. The group met every Thursday night at eight and after each session I felt like both a student and a pastor. Even after the soldiers filed out of my office, the room felt full of warmth and learning.

On Saturdays anywhere from ten to twenty-five soldiers came to my service—a good turnout for exhausted troopers who could have been catching up on sleep. Some of the soldiers kept their weapons strapped to them during sermons, others placed their weapons on the floor. There were no regulations regarding guns in the chapel. But they always took off their helmets or head gear. I was glad Seng and I had brought praise music with us, because when the soldiers sang, it took all of us out of Iraq to a much safer place in our minds.

As the situation on the ground grew more violent and complicated, my Saturday-evening sermons grew simpler and more focused. I needed to hear those sermons as much as the soldiers did. I talked about the spiritual battle believers must wage every day and how we could involve God in every aspect of our lives. I wanted my soldiers to leave the service knowing they could trust in God's unshakable character—an area in which we all needed reassurance given the circumstances.

▲▲▲

IN A FEW weeks I'd be home on leave. Bekah was waiting until a day or two before I arrived to tell the boys I was coming so they didn't get excited too early. In an e-mail to our extended family, Bekah wrote about their unique ways of showing they missed me: "Yesterday in the bath tub Blaine made up a new superhero—Coffee Man!! (Blaine loves the idea of coffee—a great treat for him is going to Starbucks, it's a special thing he does with his daddy). Tyler elaborated, 'He shoots hot coffee at the bad guys!!' Ouch!"

Every day, Bekah dealt with the challenges of having an absentee husband and father. One week, Tyler's diabetes starting acting up and she e-mailed me that he had had a seizure.

> This time the medics stayed for over an hour until he was himself again, and then treated him to seeing the inside of the ambulance. He enjoyed wearing the headphones and "talking" on the radio, wearing their fireman hat (but not running the sirens as it was 1 a.m.!)

Bekah tried to stay upbeat but I knew I was needed at home, even if just temporarily. I'd only get two weeks in Colorado, but I planned to make each day last twice as long. When I closed my eyes, I could picture holding Bekah's face in my hand, and hugging the boys so tight they'd howl.

Communications were tough. Mail was spotty (insurgents had recently fired an RPG into our mail van, setting a good number of letters and packages on fire) and Bekah and I relied mostly on e-mail. She sent me excerpts from Psalm 27:4 that were helping her cope with the constant fear of Tyler's diabetes, and which might help me with my own struggles (one of our noncommissioned officers had just been shot in the leg and it seemed each day brought a new casualty): *Honey, here's verse four, which I found fascinating. Here is David, being pursued in warfare, and what does he ask for? Not deliverance from war, not physical safety (or emotional, in my case) but this one thing— Psalm 27:4*

One thing I ask of the Lord, this is what I seek, that I may dwell in the house of the Lord all the days of my life. To gaze upon the beauty of the Lord, and to seek Him in His temple. What was the point? *Not that he would be rescued from danger,* Bekah wrote to me, *but that he would know God's presence every day.* She would have made an excellent chaplain.

7

COMFORT ZONE

Early July, in transit to Colorado
I cannot wait to see Rebekah and the boys' faces when I come
off the plane. I miss them so much and I often feel guilty
because I'm away so much. I know I am exactly where God
wants me so that is one thing that keeps me going.

WHEN I FIRST saw Rebekah at the airport, she was wearing a little black dress from our college days and had curled her hair, pinned at the sides, which I always loved. I ran over and wrapped my arms around her. She felt soft and small and her familiar scent washed over me like a tonic. I was intoxicated by a combination of the jet lag, the clamor of the families swarming around us, and the expectation of a night alone with my wife for the first time in months. Like the other soldiers, I quickly took off for home. We were all family when we were in Iraq, but when we hit the ground it was every soldier for himself.

One of Bekah's girlfriends offered to sit with the boys so we had some time alone. We both fell over each other in the car, asking questions too hard to answer quickly: How are the boys? What is Tal Afar like?

When we got home we had a few hours alone to be husband and wife again. Then the boys came rushing in just before bedtime, jumping all over me on the couch. I helped them put on their pajamas, brush their teeth, and climb into bed. I read to them from *The Very Hungry Caterpillar* and *The Monster at the End of This Book*, all the while marveling at their sweet smell and tired faces. Then I turned out the lights. Domestic bliss.

When I woke up the next morning our little townhouse felt like a resort: a comfortable bed, my beautiful wife sleeping next to me, perfect weather outside, and no plans whatsoever for the day.

Having Bekah beside me felt like a dream. There were so many times in Iraq when I couldn't call or e-mail, couldn't reach out to my wife for comfort. When someone is thousands of miles away, they sometimes stop feeling real. Now I didn't need any technology to connect with her, I only needed to let Iraq slip from my mind so that I could focus on being home.

Our bed was soft and clean and smelled of a warm dryer, not dust and grime and sweat. I knew Bekah had been cleaning like crazy, and had told her on the phone to just relax, that I didn't care about the house. But I appreciated how beautiful and orderly it looked and the effort she had made. As I lay in bed, I could feel waves of air-conditioned air washing over us every ten minutes and it felt like the soft, cool breath of angels.

We had talked on the phone a week ago about what we were missing: Bekah missed my hand on the small of her back, standing on her tiptoes so our cheeks would touch when we hugged. I'm a physical person and I told her I missed the warmth of skin—the way her face and the boys' faces felt in my hand, sensations that instant messaging and phone calls could never replace. Now, for the next two weeks I'd be able to make love to my wife, wrestle with my boys, and rest without the fear of someone knocking on my door with tragic news. There would be no constant drone of radio chatter, just laughter.

We hadn't made big plans. The boys were still young enough that any schedule revolved around early-morning naps, which kept us close to home. I also wanted to keep a low profile. In the past four months I had counseled several hundred soldiers. If I wanted to go back refreshed, I needed time with just family, not socializing.

For two days we barely left the house and I slept as much as I could. It was hard to tell whether it was the deployment, the jet lag, or the 72 hours it took me to get from Tal Afar to Colorado Springs, but those first days I felt like a character from *Star Trek*, beamed down from one alternate universe to another. At ages three and six, the boys didn't even comprehend the meaning of letting Daddy decompress. During the day time, my own home sometimes felt as overstimulating as Iraq. Bekah was equally full of energy and it was hard to match her verve. She was feeling good because she had lost the baby weight from Blaine's pregnancy and seemed to float around the house in her Capri pants and flowing blouses. As for me, each step felt like wading through mud as I shifted to the new time zone.

Bekah had arranged a special surprise: We spent two nights alone at a bed and breakfast in town. The owner served us a five-course meal in our room (everything was at a huge discount because Bekah told her I'd been in Iraq). It was bliss. Our deal was to talk about everything but Iraq and even the kids (as best we could). The aim was to forget about our cares and focus on each other before settling back into a home routine.

I'd been gone only four months but everyone seemed different. I marveled at how my family had grown without me, but was equally jealous of the time I had lost with them and nostalgic for what they had been like just before I left. I hadn't realized Blaine was already potty-trained. For weeks, if not months, I had been under orders from Bekah to tell him I used the bathroom every morning, and I had been dutifully reporting my morning routine. Last I had heard, he was in diapers, talking about being an "Army man like Daddy." I guess I had missed his big turning point.

As for Tyler, he was gearing up to start first grade. He wanted to be like the other kids and not always stop in the middle of play for blood-sugar checkups. He had begun rebelling against Bekah, and I had a talk with him about how important it was for him to care for his health and to listen to his mom. I'm not sure I made any headway, but Bekah was appreciative. He also needed help with his handwriting, which was almost impossible to read. I sat down with him and we wrote out some letters; Bekah had been urging him to slow down, and I tried the same technique. His kindergarten teacher worried it was all the needle pricks on his fingers from the glucometer. I figured it was impatience and knew exactly where that trait came from.

The boys just seemed to be growing up so fast, and I was missing it all.

One day Bekah wanted to break out of the house, to take the boys to a downtown playground with a water fountain for them to splash in. We got them dressed in their T-shirts, swimsuits, and plastic swimming shoes. We were all looking forward to a day in the sun when I realized it was Saturday and that the playground would be packed. Suddenly, I felt an odd, electric tingling run through my body and my stomach sank.

"I think it might be too crowded," I told Bekah hesitantly, as she always hated last-minute changes in plan. "Maybe it would be better to just spend time as a family, not surrounded by strangers?" But the boys were already in their swimsuits, she said, which meant it would be a struggle to talk them out of swimming. She knew of another fountain, but this one was across town, 40 minutes away. She sounded disappointed, the closer fountain was the boy's new favorite, but within a few minutes we were on our way to the second choice.

Bekah knew the way so she drove us on a four-lane highway with endless traffic lights, all red. I realized I wasn't used to riding in a vehicle without a convoy to back me up and didn't like idling too long at stoplights. Our van was what in Iraq we'd call a "soft-skinned vehicle" and I felt as exposed in it as if I were driving naked. I scanned everything around us for potential danger. That trash at the side of the road? Who knew what was hidden under it. I asked her to switch lanes. Cars following too close behind us? Suspicious, so I'd urge her to switch lanes again. It was exhausting, Bekah was annoyed, and I suddenly found myself longing for the safety of Seng's protection.

By the time we parked and walked to the fountain, I had relaxed, but now the boys didn't want to get wet. They kept arguing about which one could climb on my shoulders, but since Blaine couldn't pronounce the word "shoulders" he kept saying he wanted to ride on my "soldiers." We laughed it all off, had some ice cream, and left. But we stayed closer to home after that.

I pulled the boys in a wagon to the playgrounds on post, and chased them mercilessly. When I needed time to myself, I'd go to my favorite Starbucks in downtown Colorado Springs to read and drink what I could never, ever replicate with my chapel coffeemaker—Grande Nonfat Caramel Macchiatos. I was having a slightly hard time adjusting to the time difference because of nightmares, of all things, and the coffee helped.

Mid-July 2005
I'm at my "sanctuary" downtown. They've rearranged things and made it more modern, but this is still my place to recharge and read. I've been home for a week now and it has been nice to relax and not be tied to a schedule. I cannot say that it has been a restful week because going back is always on my mind. I've had three bad dreams the last several

nights about "letting others down" or "failing" in my re-
sponsibilities. I am anxious about the next 7 months and
what I will be like upon my return.

In my nightmares I would rush into army tents, ready
to help with a catastrophe, only to find out everyone had
already left, usually for a mission I hadn't been informed
of. I wasn't needed. At night I dreamed about failing in
the Army, and by day, surrounded by civilians, I dreamed
about leaving the Army.

I looked up from my journal and watched the people
in Starbucks. That's when the reality of my life really
started to sink in. Did any of these people understand
what was happening in Iraq? Looking around, you'd
never know there was a war going on. There was no ra-
tioning of foodstuffs to support the troops, no American
flags flying proudly in storefronts. The people surrounding me didn't seem to know they were just one airplane
trip away from a world where your boots were always
coated with sand and your mind was constantly drenched
with fear.

The longer I sat there the harder it became to
tell which felt less real—Starbucks or Tal Afar. At that
moment they both felt like something out of a strange
fairy tale.

Maybe these people here had it right. What was I
thinking, going off to Iraq without a weapon when I had
a family and obligations here at home? I could shut Iraq
out of my mind just like others seemed to. Why didn't I
just let myself do that?

▲▲▲

BEKAH UNDERSTOOD THAT I just wanted to stay home
and avoid large groups, but she was also getting worried
that I wasn't recharging spiritually during my break from
duty. If anyone knew how to keep me on my path, it was
Bekah.

Back in college I had signed up for the Bible study
class she led each week at the Baptist Student Union. The
group of us, about ten to twenty students, would talk
about stressors in our lives, from flunking tests and parents getting divorced to how to live for God. Bekah
helped us navigate the good and the bad as the year
progressed.

We had been like a tag team when it came to faith.
She brought me to her Bible studies and I brought her
deeper into involvement with our local church, encour-
aging her to join events with the community at large, not
just those designed for students. We grew deeper in our
faith together, and it was Bekah who knew I was called
into ministry before I did. After eighteen months I proposed. She had always thought she would marry a mis-
sionary, but my seeking the ministry seemed to be close
enough. Still, she was nervous. The morning after I proposed she did what she always did, spent some quiet time
in prayer. It was in that quiet hour that she felt that God
confirmed to her that He would be with us, and we've
been together ever since.

Since then, with the long deployments and the stress
of two small children, she often returned to that moment

to regain her composure. She understood that deploy-ments could drain that life out of a person, and that I also needed anchoring during my time at home. So, as she had done over a decade ago, she asked me to attend some Bible studies.

We went to a Bible study at the home of Mike Barry, a fellow chaplain who served at Fort Carson and lived just two blocks away. There were about eight of us there, mostly couples, and by now I was feeling happy to be out of the house. Just before we started, Mike turned to me to say he was sorry about the two deaths from my squadron. What deaths? I asked. He wasn't sure. He had only heard that two soldiers were killed the past Saturday and didn't know anything else. I could feel my heart sink and my stomach churn. Like the soldiers in so many debriefing sessions, I felt the guilt starting to flood in. I wasn't there for my soldiers. I trained with them, invested blood and tears with them. I wanted to be there with them in this time of grief. That was my job.

I couldn't focus on the rest of the Bible study. My mind was back in the desert and my heart and body felt as heavy as if weighted down with body armor. Who was killed? Different faces flashed into my mind. What hap-pened? Why didn't someone from my unit contact me? Why didn't I get a heads-up from Chaplain Causey?

I rushed home and quickly fired up the computer to check e-mail. Anxiety pulsed through my entire body as I scanned the subject headers in my in-box. An Amazon order for Erik H. Erikson's *Identity and the Life Cycle* had been processed. A few friends were asking how my leave was going. But that was it. Maybe Rebekah could help. "Wait, honey," I said as I caught her walking upstairs to the kids. "What's the password to your Hotmail account?" Perhaps the Family Readiness Group leader, my squadron commander's wife, would have sent something to the squadron wives about the event. The FRG is a support group for spouses, and it delivers the first news about the deaths of soldiers after their families are officially notified.

Bekah came over and helped sift through her e-mail, finally finding what appeared to be the notification. I opened up the message and sped through it. Two deaths had been announced, and they were from my squadron. I froze when I read the second name. Bekah looked at me. "I should be there," was all I could say. She tried to console me but the boys were crying out from upstairs, so she let me be.

The details were worse than I could have imagined. A medic in my squadron had been racing to a Forward Aid Station, carrying an injured private first class, when the vehicle was struck by an rocket-propelled grenade. Both men died when the vehicle flipped over. The injured soldier was Brady Westin.

I turned my eyes from the computer screen and stared at our dining room wall, which soon seemed to be closing in on me. I remembered how closely Chaplain Bixler and I had worked with Brady. I remembered the four months of counseling him between deployments, the PTSD symptoms, and his guilt over killing an Iraqi insurgent who was aiming at him. He had married and was on track to a better life, trying to shake his fear from the first deployment. His wife was expecting their first child.

I had seen Brady just a week earlier at the Support Squadron Aid Station. He was suffering from heat exhaustion after helping to evacuate a soldier who had been injured during a raid. He looked worn out, his hair was disheveled, and his uniform was covered with dirt, but despite his emotional conflicts, he always remained a tough and loyal soldier. Looking back, it was hard to accept that this was the last time I'd ever see him.

I felt like I had just lost a family member. I sent out so many e-mails asking for information I'm surprised my computer didn't crash. Chaplain Causey was one of the first to respond.

> Roger: These things will happen, so please devote this time to your family. The Army has too much of you as it is.

He went on to explain the details of the deaths and mentioned that Brady's platoon had a 30 percent casualty rate and many were going on a five-day leave to Qatar because they were reaching a breaking point. He closed by saying,

> Now, please, forget about us. We knew things like this would happen. When I'm gone I'll need you to cover for me. You are the only advocate Rebekah and the boys have. So give this time to them. God bless you guys. We're fine here.

The next person I wanted to hear from was Maria. She would give me the details Chaplain Causey had left out. I suddenly missed her, but not in a romantic way, it was more like missing a sister. Bekah once remarked that I had a habit of seeking father and sister figures, and had always tried to instill in me the idea that I would be happiest if I relied on God to fill some of the deeper voids in my life, not just friends and family. She was right. But at the same time my bond with Maria was necessary; she was my only partner for stress debriefings and the only official mental health counselor on the base. It was true I had always related better to women than men, perhaps because my father was so absent during my childhood. But out of necessity the physical and emotional turmoil Maria and I endured in Iraq created an airtight bond between us.

Maria wrote a few hours later.

Hey—you are supposed to be enjoying your leave. Yes, unfortunately, there were 2-KIAs and one soldier is still in critical condition. I had seen Brady the Saturday prior so this one really hit home. When I first heard it didn't click, but an hour before I was to facilitate the debriefing, it all clicked and I cried during the entire thing. Though I had only seen him that once, he spoke to me in length about his first deployment, his PTSD and how excited he was to go on leave soon to see his son born. I apologized to the soldiers, but they stated they understood. The memorial was yesterday and it did provide me some closure, but it's still hard.

That night I was torn between two families. One was in the other room, where Rebekah was getting the boys ready for sleep, brushing their teeth and cajoling them to "go potty." They had created their own little world during my absences and as much as they missed me, they seemed to cope without me. My other family was 7,000 miles away in a miserable desert, suffering and in grave danger. That was the family I needed to be with at that moment, but I was unable to help them from my cozy town home. My whole leave suddenly felt unreal, as if Colorado was a dream and I would wake up back in my bed at the chapel office any minute now.

How had I, just a few days earlier, sat in Starbucks and considered leaving the Army? I was horrified with myself and felt like a traitor. I needed to get back to Iraq to be surrounded by other soldiers' discipline, purpose, and faith in mission. I wanted to be there for the soldiers, to jump back into the cycle of chaos I had grown accustomed to, even if that meant I'd have to leave Bekah and my sons again. I had enough training as a pastor and chaplain to know this way of thinking was risky, but at that moment the last person I was worried about was myself.

8

▲▲▲

DRAINING THE POND

Late July 2005
Well, I am on the plane and we are about to take off. I must not lose sight of the goals: Draw closer to God, develop my person, be consistent and disciplined in my faith, don't shirk my duties, and be a committed father and husband. If I can do these things I will be on the right path. God can fill the voids in my life, we do not have to depend on others to supply what is missing from our lives. It is taking two deployments to Iraq and a lot of grace from God to see what I am starting to see.

I am ready to get back and finish what I started. I am ready to be my unit's chaplain.

BY EARLY AUGUST our troops had fully secured Tal Afar's police station, fort, and hospital. But the trouble spots were only growing more troublesome. We had learned that bin Laden's man in Iraq—Abu Mousab al-Zarqawi—was commanding local units right under our noses,

turning Tal Afar into an ever-stronger center of gun trafficking and propaganda for the insurgency. Rebels were
videotaping battles with our soldiers, and Tal Afar featured heavily in the "top 10 attacks" tape circulated
among insurgent groups. The thought of our soldiers'
deaths caught on video, as a source of viewing pleasure,
made me sick.

Once again I convoyed out with our medics to set up
a Forward Aid Station. This time we headed to Tal Afar's
granary, where we would receive wounded soldiers from
the day's mission to sweep several city neighborhoods.
The medics parked the vehicles so that a tarp could be
strung between them for shade, but it was close to 120
degrees out and we were baking. As I looked over the
gurneys and oxygen tanks and—so far—empty stretchers,
I prayed that this would not turn out to be a bad day for
our troops. It was midmorning, and in the distance I
could hear our Howitzers firing into the forest just outside town, trying to harass the insurgents and let them
know Big Brother was watching.

I walked inside the granary. Until recently it had been
used by local farmers to store their crops, now it stood
empty. Its concrete cylinder mills rose more than 100 feet
in the air and I started walking up the stairs inside one of
them to get what I was always seeking, a better view of
the situation, a fleeting sense of control in this godfor-
saken place. It was dark in the stairwell, and with all
my protective gear—interceptor armor, flame-resistant
gloves, ballistic goggles, and chaplain's kits—I was carrying an extra 30 pounds. At the top several soldiers had
taken up machine-gun positions in a hangarlike room

with antiquated motors, exposed pipes, and broken windows. Earlier that day there had been a Special Forces sniper positioned in the room and he must have smashed out some of the glass.

I made my way to a corner window and saw smoke rising from what we called the forest, the patch of trees and foliage that had sprouted where the city sewage drained away. I finally had some perspective; looking through the shattered glass with the warm air hitting my face reminded me of the hot Texas afternoons of my childhood. In the distance I spotted an M1A2 Abrams battle tank silently creeping along a neighborhood street. A moment later I heard it blast its main gun, a 120-mm heat round, and a second later half of the home in front of it had collapsed.

A woman and two little children ran from the rubble. My God. I had seen tanks fire, but I had never seen one take out a house, especially at such close range. It didn't seem like a location for insurgents. The smoke cleared and I stared at the scene below me in shock. What prompted that tank to fire? The mother and children running—this wasn't right.

When I was in seminary, the questions I struggled with most were those related to justice and fairness. How can God direct one group of people to exterminate another group? How, after seeing what war does to people, can God allow it continue? "Do not murder" is a fundamental lesson of the Bible. Yet it is one of its more confusing teachings. In the book of Joshua, God tells the Israelites to wipe out everyone in Canaan, including the children and even the animals. In the book of Exodus,

God hardens Pharoah's heart to the point of having him send a death angel to wipe out all the first-born children of Egypt. How does God determine who is just, or who has the right to judge and therefore to kill?

I hoped that as a military chaplain, I could work in a war zone and in a small way try to mitigate the toll that war takes on people. To stop wider bloodshed or tragedy, it was best, I figured, to start with individuals and help them find their own stability and be anchored in their spirituality. If I felt a soldier was thinking of revenge or was angry or distraught, I would talk with them until they cooled off, or would ask them if they wanted me to have a superior pull them from immediate duty so they'd have some time to recover. We're not designed, as humans, to naturally handle the violence of war. I thought I would understand more about war and faith and humanity the more I was involved; instead it was the opposite. For someone like me, who understood that life was hardly black and white, the gray areas of the Bible and the gray areas of Iraq were nonetheless becoming a lesson in confusion, not in faith.

Standing by the window, I realized my uniform was soaked with sweat; I had been in my armored vest for at least 10 hours. I knew we would be receiving casualties soon, so I walked down from the granary and toward the medics' area. As I suspected, we had received a ground MEDEVAC call in reference to some civilians whose roof had caved in.

The medic track soon arrived and unloaded a baby, a toddler, and two adults, their clothes torn and covered in dirt. I didn't know if they came from the same house I had seen destroyed. The mother and father were sobbing as their infant was placed on one stretcher, their four-year-old on another. The main doctor on duty, by some miracle, had a pediatric specialty and he started checking the small body for wounds. There was blood covering the front of what looked like a tiny white nightgown. Perhaps the baby was a girl. I spoke to her in my best daddy voice and tried to hold her squirming hand. Her high-pitched screams sounded like justified accusations. I felt my eyes tearing up as the parents continued to cry and speak in Arabic, which none of us understood. There were no translators in sight.

Mid-August 2005
I don't have a desire to totally give myself to God. However, I am praying that God changes my desire. I am listening to the Bible on CD and it is hard to believe that Paul would devote his whole life to God. It almost sounds one-dimensional. I struggle with this because I know that I will always struggle in ministry if I don't devote my whole life to God.

In the midst of the daily violence I received some good news about my future: I had just been accepted for a Clinical Pastoral Education Residency, a special training to work inside army, not just civilian, hospitals. I was excited by the challenge. I'd always been drawn to grief ministry because it forced me to focus on the basics: What does it mean to live and what does it mean to die? I'd study at one of four leading army hospitals, work toward a Doctorate in Ministry degree, and then spend three years working in an army hospital. I didn't know which hospital I'd train at, but being in the program meant I wouldn't redeploy to Iraq for more than four years. I hoped for all our sakes that the war would be over by then.

A few days after I announced the good news, Seng walked into our chapel office with a grim expression and a sheet of paper in hand. He had just visited our supervisory chaplain and noticed a troubling official memo about me on his desk, snatched it, and brought it for me to see. This didn't sound good. What had I done wrong?

I saw the subject line and was confused; my superior chaplain wanted me removed from the program I'd just been accepted to. But halfway through the e-mail I started to laugh.

REVOCATION OF PARTICIPATION IN CLINICAL PASTORAL EDUCATION FOR CHAPLAIN ROGER BENIMOFF.

1. I urgently recommend the immediate removal of Chaplain Benimoff from the CPE OML due to serious violations of Army policies and unethical practices.

2. It is with deep regret that I must inform you that Chaplain Benimoff has a serious chemical addiction and has the reputation among his soldiers and peers as the "squadron coffee fiend." His personal fetish for Starbucks is especially alarming.

3. I also find it unacceptable that any chaplain in the US Army should bear the nickname "Sticky Fingers." But Chaplain Benimoff has earned this title, and glories in it. Whether it is from my personal stash of goodies

sent from my wife or from the care packages sent by hardworking Americans to the soldiers in the trenches—it all ends up in Chaplain Benimoff's stomach. When I confronted him for helping himself to the contents of care packages, he responded to my face with these words: "Hey, I'm worth it." The man is out of control. When he should be hanging his head in shame, instead he bee-bops along singing the Journey tune, "Be Good to Yourself, Nobody Else Will."

4. I therefore strongly urge that his name be removed from the CPE OML. I would especially appreciate this since his cockiness about his selection for CPE training is really beginning to bug me.

DAVID C. CAUSEY
Chaplain (MAJ), USA
Regimental Chaplain

Seng was trying not to laugh—he had me for a while there. It was clear that my coffee addiction had become quite notorious. There was that time, after all, that my coffee grinder broke. Every day for a month Seng had to watch me put coffee beans in a towel, roll it up, and then smack it with a hammer, so I guess I deserved the ridicule.

Bekah was thrilled that I'd gotten into the hospital training program. Even though the deployments were an expected part of life, there was no denying that they strained our marriage. As I advised other married soldiers to do, Bekah and I were now instant messaging as often as we could. It was helping us break out of our pattern of businesslike e-mails, but stress levels were high both in Colorado, where Tyler had just started school and Bekah was straining to manage his diabetes, and for me here in Tal Afar, where every day felt like an exhausting race with no finish line in sight.

> *Mid-August 2005*
> *I'm not sure exactly what is happening within me. I have become almost agoraphobic and I leave my office only when necessary. I am very uncomfortable (emotionally) and I am sick of this. Every day is the same and I am not even sure that I will be happy back home. Tyler's diabetes, redeployment, and Rebekah all combine to create a very demanding environment. I'm not sure if I have the ability to manage these aspects and also manage myself. I cannot remember functioning being so difficult.*

In late August a sniper shot and killed one of our men, Sergeant Lugo, at an outpost in the city. I stood with the soldiers as their commanders gave them the news. Some of the soldiers listened passively. Others cried. It felt like Groundhog Day; this was happening all too often. But this time, I didn't feel one step removed, a calm presence walking with the soldiers in their grief. I was one of them, hearing the news and numbly staring ahead. Just a few days earlier I had stood outside a tank at the exact location where he was shot. It was harder to counsel when I knew it could have been me, that I had been so naive when the possible consequences were so real.

The day after Lugo was killed, another soldier was

killed in the same location, as was a pilot providing backup. Our superiors guessed it was the same sniper who got both soldiers on the ground, perhaps a foreign fighter due to his excellent aim and superb weapon handling.

About 5 minutes before I was to give the invocation for Lugo's memorial service, I looked into the sky as the sun was setting, usually my favorite time of day. A C130 cargo plane was flying past, which meant that the ramp ceremonies for the other two departed soldiers must have just finished. I knew it was carrying two flag-draped caskets across the horizon. It also meant that after the memorial ceremony for Lugo, whose body had already been flown out, it would be only 24 hours before I'd attend another service for the fallen.

The stress on our squadrons was mounting and my own workload was piling up. That month I would conduct three stress debriefings for 33 soldiers, make 440 individual soldier visits, conduct 12 Word of the Day sessions for 415 soldiers, and hold 2 memorial services with 500 soldiers in attendance.

Most of the time I was absorbed in and proud of my work. But there were brief, darker moments when I felt like I was part of a giant assembly line. The line started with a walking, talking young man, his mind and soul devoted to a noble cause. In the beginning, he was dressed in a uniform and given a gun. Further down the line he was lying on a stretcher, his uniform scissored open by medics. Then there were the assembly-line casket workers. Near the end of the line, there was me, the sensitive one who walked the remaining soldiers through their

grief, the Hero Flight, and, finally, the memorial ceremony. At these dark moments it was hard for me to reconcile a benevolent God; with the reality on the ground I
could only think about this terrible machinery of death
and wonder why no one seemed capable of turning it off.

▲▲▲

IN ONE 24-hour-period we shipped three bodies back to
Colorado, spreading chaos there.

Two of the dead had lived on our street in Fort Carson, and both wives were notified on the same day. As
Bekah pulled into our driveway that evening with a car
full of groceries, a friend immediately dashed over and
gave her the news. The neighborhood sprung into action;
name plates on the two homes were taken down in order
to divert any local press, casseroles were in the ovens,
everyone jumped in. In the days that followed, Bekah, a
board member at our church on post, became the go-be-
tween for the families and the congregation. Friends of
the widows would call Bekah and explain what was
needed: perhaps a meal, or—at one point—no more
meals; a prayer request; or, later, a request not to stand in
groups crying in the front yard.

Soon Bekah was e-mailing me for counseling advice.
The domino effect of the deaths always lasted long beyond what the news cycle would have people believe.
Friends of the wives, she said, were feeling their own survivor's guilt, having not lost their husbands. Families
were uprooted: after the deaths, the widows often left the
base to be closer to their families, and this severed friend-

ships. Before one widow moved she gave Bekah her son's twin-sized bed, which was shaped like a racing car. It would fit Tyler perfectly and she couldn't take it with her. Even today, Bekah will pray for her when she tucks Tyler into bed at night, remembering how even in her grief this mother had made the effort to pass on a gift.

▲▲▲

THE REGIMENT HAD had enough. Operation Restoring Rights was launched on September 2. It was to be the largest urban assault since the siege of Fallujah. In previous operations, our soldiers would fight in town, then retreat back to the base. That strategy had been flawed. Now they would move in and stay in. Five thousand U.S. and Iraqi troops entered Tal Afar before dawn. After circling the city with troops, the next step was to get the civilians out of town by ordering families out of their homes, often by gunpoint, to temporary camps just outside the city limits.

Once the civilians were rounded out, the next step was to go after the insurgents. The troops infiltrated the city and worked in small squads of ten to fifteen soldiers, leaping from roof to roof to avoid booby-trapped streets. They had serious backup: Air Force fighter jets to drop laser-guided bombs on "hot" locations, an Air Force C130 gunship, our own internal Apache and Kiowa Scout helicopters with 2.75-inch rockets, .50-caliber machine guns, and Hellfire missiles.

In all my army years I had never seen such an armada assembled for one mission. I was torn. On one hand I was deeply troubled by this machinery of death, yet another side of me was filled with pride for being part of an operation designed to completely rid a city of insurgents who had terrorized the local population. My mission for the week was to travel to all of the second squadron outposts to minister to troops before heading back to Camp Sykes. Heavy Company, the 43rd Engineers, Eagle, Fox, and Grim Troops were all headed into the city to set up outposts, and I'd travel with them to counsel.

Ministering in a war zone often happens in short, unanticipated snatches of time. During preps for the operation, a private, Doug Byrd, motioned me into the cab of his 5-ton vehicle, its noisy, idling motor creating a makeshift wall of privacy between us and his fellow troops. He was distraught over a supervisor demeaning him in front of the other troops. We pulled his sergeant over to talk it through and wrapped up with a pledge from both sides to cooperate. A few months later I would get a knock on my chapel door at 2:00 a.m. telling me Byrd had died of pneumonia.

We knew that over the next few weeks roughing it would be the norm. Soldiers had their gear and their cots, and would be living in tough conditions—barely edible Ready To Eat Meals, only one hot meal a day, and no air conditioning in the 120-degree heat. I too was geared up in my full "battle rattle": my vest, Kevlar gloves, goggles, camouflage backpack, and chaplain's kits. I threw in a roll of toilet paper, some counseling books, and hand gel. In my chaplain's kits as always I had my shoal, communion wafers, cans of grape juice, a metal cross, and metal chalice for communion. I also cut Word of the Day messages into small strips like in fortune cookies. I passed them out to soldiers, who'd sometimes carry them in their wallets or paste them up in their tanks. I had everything I could possibly need.

Early September 2005

Today we are in the midst of a regimental battle in the "Saria" district of Tal Afar. I'm with Grim Troop in an abandoned school and I can hear gunfire. I like being close to the battle even though there is some risk. If Rebekah knew, she wouldn't be happy. We have been hitting the AIF (anti-Iraqi Forces) hard over the last three days. We have about seven more days of this and then we will head back to Camp Sykes. It has been a while since I have roughed it. But I can get used to this. At first I was dreading this, but I have been able to travel and get a different perspective of battle. The funny thing is that I'm not afraid. I almost want to get shot at. It is an adrenalin rush being on the "front lines." I am among some of the bravest people I have known: First Sergeant Serrano, Captain Howell, and others who daily risk their lives.

I had convoyed into the infamous Saria district, Tal Afar's most dangerous, in the back of an Armored Personnel Carrier with Grim Troop. We'd just come from a combat outpost where our engineer company tested an explosive device, showering dirt and debris all over our heads and terrifying us because we had missed the warning. Then we convoyed in to Saria, broke through a wall surrounding an abandoned school with a tank, and set up position in the building for the first of what would be many nights outside the wire. I had spent the afternoon laying sandbags against the school windows and now we were finally turning in for a few hours.

As always, our personal lives are what most often occupy our minds, even in war zones. Captain Howell had set up his sleeping quarters in a small schoolroom, surrounded by desks and easels, and on this and future visits he let me crash with him. In that dusty room he confided in me that he was worried about his upcoming wedding, that maybe he wasn't really ready to get married. As we fell asleep I asked him to remember what it was he loved about his fiancée, Renee, and why he had proposed. We'd repeat this conversation many times over the coming months as I visited him outside the wire and he would eventually ask me to conduct the wedding after we all got home. We rarely talked about religion; Howell had grown up in a devout Southern Baptist household but over time had become jaded about faith. Losing so many of his soldiers only solidified his distaste for the promise that someone was watching over him. So most nights, against the backdrop of gunfire, we discussed relationships, not God. A few weeks later he asked me if I'd conduct his wedding; I said I'd be honored to.

Meanwhile, he and his soldiers were going 100 miles an hour trying to secure the school and conduct patrols. Their time was tight; I held brief, 12-minute-long worship services for them and led just a handful of praise songs. One evening as Seng and I were "fellowshipping"— shooting the breeze—with some of the soldiers in a bas-

ketball court behind the school, we heard shots ring out
in our direction. The incoming rounds started without
warning, and all that Seng and I had time to do was duck.
The other soldiers were faster and had dashed into a
nearby schoolroom. After a few minutes we raced across
the court to join them until we got the radio all-clear
from soldiers scouting the perimeter of the school. I
wasn't scared, I was more in shock, and it was only when
I climbed into my cot later that night that I remembered
it was my birthday.

After several days with Grim Troop, Seng and I
moved to Fox Troop's outpost where Maria was already
counseling troops. On our first day with Fox Troop, we
had some rare downtime, so the three of us played Spades
with some of the soldiers. That would soon become our
trademark for the rest of the deployment. Maria began
carrying two packs of cards, scorecards, and pencils wher-
ever she went, and when soldiers in the outposts saw us
coming, they'd always want to "beat the chaplain and the
lady social worker." We had earned a reputation as fierce
players and trash talkers, "We're not only here to counsel
you, but here to rip you," we'd warn them. They dished
right back, and since the outpost soldiers didn't have
electronics, the cards were a special hit. It was a great way
to build rapport and drain stress.

Later that night some other Fox Troop soldiers took
us up to the roof of a building they were guarding. We
laid down on cots that had been lined up under a breezeway, looking up at the starry night peppered with Hellfire
missiles that sent flashes of blue and white lights into the
sky. That night we felt like we were witnessing history in

the making. We would later learn that many of Zarqawi's insurgents had slipped away and that their safe houses and weapons caches had been cleansed after a pause in fighting was called for by the Iraqi government. We had made serious inroads, but the story of Tal Afar after the offensive would later be described by one embedded reporter as "a parable of the dangers, dilemmas and frustrations that still haunt the U.S. in Iraq."

What struck me sitting there on that roof, however, was that I was starting to abandon all fear. We heard tanks firing their guns and for some reason I felt calm, even though I wasn't wearing a vest or a helmet; I was wearing shorts and flip-flops. Something had clicked. I felt I had gained a form of immunity from the violence surrounding me.

▲▲▲

9

CRASH LANDING

Mid-October 2005
I traveled every day this last week. We had two suicide
bombings in two days and Maria and I have been traveling
to critical incident debriefings. It is quite disorienting to
adapt to the chaotic environment here and think about the
rest of life. So many have been killed & injured.

I had a counseling session with Sergeant Greene. When
he came in, he was ready to leave his wife for having an
emotional affair with another man. But what he was saying
was incongruent with his nonverbals. . . . He left with a
more realistic view of the problem and his feelings &
thoughts. I tried not to fill in the blanks for him because self-
discovery is key. I merely tried to be a "tour guide" who
drove him to different sites than previously seen or viewed. I
know without a doubt that God has gifted me in this area.

Also conducted a debriefing for Heavy. Sergeant Miller
was injured and I saw the damage to the Hummer. It was

really bad. Blood all over the vehicle and shrapnel holes in it.
The driver's door was destroyed and the glass was broken
through. It's so hard seeing people I know sustain injuries.

THE NEXT TIME I saw Miller, his chin was still bandaged
and he had to talk from the side of his mouth. With five
words he managed to describe perfectly the reality of life
outside the wire. "Chaplain," he told me, "it's not *if*; it's
when."

Before the September offensive, I had made only occasional trips into Tal Afar. Now I spent half my week
convoying to our small combat outposts in town. Despite
the dangers, I preferred to be outside the wire. I loved
walking around the combat outposts and talking with soldiers about everything from their marriages to their fears
being out in the field to what passages they might find
helpful in the Bible. I felt like I blended in, as if Tal Afar
was somehow where I now belonged.

At the end of each week I'd return to Camp Sykes for
counseling, to catch up on paperwork, and to conduct
Saturday-evening services. Even though I enjoyed the
travel to outposts, the camp began to feel like the pinnacle of civilization. The food was hot, and now that Seng
found a mattress for me I slept every night in a bed with
actual sheets and blankets. I had the luxury of an office
door, one I could shut, creating a silent chamber that
protected me from the maelstrom outside. But I couldn't
stay at camp too long. I wanted to be a presence to the
soldiers and I wasn't about to be branded by the combat
guys as a "FOBBIT," someone who never left the For-

ward Operating Base, FOB. As soon as I got too comfortable, I went right back out again.

In one month alone there were four suicide bombings
in Tal Afar. Thirty-six Iraqis were killed, almost a hundred were injured, and it was our soldiers who handled
the cleanup. There was no letup and as the weeks progressed it was getting harder for me to hear their stories.
There was so much death, and it became more difficult
for me to put my faith in God. I felt like I needed something concrete and real to support me, and prayer didn't
feel all that real lately. Maybe, like all of us on the base, I
just needed some sleep. I'm just overwhelmed, I thought.
This will pass.

We held two debriefings for suicide bombings in a
single day.

One soldier saw the body of an Iraqi girl flung over
the roof of a building; another said that the smell of
burning flesh would keep him from eating meat for the
rest of his life. Others talked of helping men search the
marketplace for the body parts of their wives, hoping to
piece them back together so the women could be buried
in one piece. "It didn't bother me at all," said one soldier
in his late teens. "Better the Iraqis than us . . . if they want
to kill each other off, that's fine by me." I had a strong
suspicion that this soldier was just putting up a tough
front, but it was getting harder for any of us to make
sense of our emotions.

That month there were two debriefings for Lion
Battery, two for Fox Troop, and one for Heavy Company, all related to the suicide bombings. Seng, Maria,

and I would convoy to various outposts in and around Tal Afar for the sessions. Sometimes we would fly in Black-hawks to remote locations and then camp out in the evenings under the stars, listening to jazz on Maria's tiny CD player to decompress. On these nights the movie cameras of our minds may have been filled with images from our sessions with soldiers, images of dead girls draped on rooftops and mothers screaming over bloodied infants, but our conversation stayed rigidly focused on small talk.

Avoidance of trauma takes many forms, from small talk and jokes to the simple act of just giving up. At some point or other, fear is a part of all of our lives, not just those of us in war. With the combination of Tyler's diabetes seizures and my absence, Bekah was also overwhelmed. In an e-mail she explained how she was also trying to let go of her constant fear of losing our son. "When his blood glucose is too high or too low, I have to choose to surrender to God and pray and let go and resist all fear," she wrote. Sometimes fear is so great, a person just has to abandon it.

Back in Iraq I saw this in myself and in the soldiers when they stood out in the open for too long. They were tired of hiding; it was complete and pure surrender— to God, to fate, or just to exhaustion. Things got easier once you gained immunity, once you detached from your fear.

Even I sometimes fantasized about getting killed in action; much better to go out with a bang. If it boiled down to "not if, but when" then, why not? Give yourself over to God. Give yourself over to someone else, whomever it is.

There were three months left to our deployment and my squadron's morale was low. Conditions were harsh and there was no letup in combat operations. So Maria, Seng, and I tried to help them in every small way we could, even when some of the commanders deeply distrusted our ability to make a difference. Grim Troop's 1st Sgt. Freddy Serrano didn't want to like me. The chaplain for his men during our first deployment had been fired for inappropriate behavior, and at the start of the deployment Serrano's first words to me, in his thick Puerto Rican accent, were gruff: "Prove to me you're a good chaplain." But Serrano soon realized that I would love him and his soldiers no matter what he said or asked for. I organized care packages for his troops, helped serve chow for them, and—perhaps since I had been enlisted as a fuel specialist long before becoming a chaplain—was no stranger to grunt work and always offered to help.

One night at midnight Maria, Seng, and I drove in a tank to Fort Tal Afar to deliver mint–chocolate chip ice cream to the soldiers there. Maria had asked them what they wanted most and that's what they had asked for— thinking it was a mission impossible. Little did they know who they were dealing with. We carried a five-gallon tub that was frozen solid when we left Camp Sykes. After an hour in the tank, it had almost turned to soup, but we managed to get it to their makeshift freezer and serve it to them the next day. It was a creature comfort, but with the heat and rough conditions, it was the first luxury they'd had in weeks. The three of us were proud of our-selves for being able to pull something off for the troops that had a visible effect on their mood. Lately it seemed hard to do it any other way.

▲▲▲

THE GRANARY WAS still a trouble spot. One day in No-vember Fox Troop informed me that a soldier there needed urgent counseling and that they had a convoy ready to escort me from the camp. I told Seng to prepare our Hummer and his equipment. Because of the security logistics involved the trip could take up to five hours, even though the granary was only a few kilometers away. Then Seng and I would come right back to camp to finish preparing for Saturday's contemporary service, one that involves more upbeat praise and worship songs, instead of traditional hymns. I was worried about handling both the trip and the service, but as soon as I pulled on my in-terceptor armor vest, shatter-resistant goggles, and com-bat helmet, I felt charged up and filled with a sense of mission.

At the granary I was introduced to Pvt. Leonard Smith, a skinny young soldier who looked quietly agi-tated. We found two chairs and pulled them to the center of the granary's makeshift gym, which was nearly empty save for a few free weights. Smith and his tank crew had been involved in a dangerous house raid that had turned physical several days earlier. They were searching an in-surgent's home when a crowd of Iraqi men gathered out-side and he and his crew had to force their way back through the mob to reach their tank. I encouraged him to talk about his anxiety over almost firing a first shot into what appeared to be an unarmed crowd. He was angry that his crew had been so exposed, in danger, and had no backup. We talked for nearly an hour before shaking hands and agreeing to meet again. I convoyed back to the relative safety of Camp Sykes to work on that night's sermon, wanting to follow up with him soon.

Several hours after our talk, Smith and his team were called in as backup for an incident in town. En route they rolled over an IED, which breached the hull of their tank. Their gunner was killed instantly. Both the platoon sergeant and the private I had counseled, Smith, had severe leg and hip injuries.

I got another chaplain to take over my service and in no time I was in a Blackhawk with our regimental commander, Col. H.R. McMaster and other command members flying to the army hospital in Mosul. McMaster was stocky, with a shaved head and a tough demeanor. He was in charge of the entire Third Armored Cavalry and despite his heavy schedule would always bring a team of officers and a chaplain to visit soldiers when they had been wounded. I rarely saw my soldiers after they had been medically evacuated, though, and was looking forward to the chance to minister to them.

"How are you holding up, Chaplain?" McMaster asked me on the helicopter. He said he knew this must be hard on me and that he appreciated my work. I wasn't about to tell him I didn't want to leave my office some days and that I was so exhausted, I often couldn't think straight.

I told him I was doing fine.

We landed and quickly walked into a large room filled with gurneys and medical equipment. I was still wearing all my body armor, but held my helmet under my arm. I felt grateful that my senior command respected the troop's need for pastoral care and that McMaster made it a point to visit every injured soldier.

I saw Smith in a corner of the room. A few hours earlier I had been counseling him and now he was drugged beyond consciousness and rigged up to an IV. I swallowed hard and walked toward his bed. I stopped, put my hand on his shoulder, introduced myself to him again, and prayed for him. His eyes were partially open. I don't know if he heard or saw me, but I looked into his eyes in the hope that the human contact would somehow break through the drugs and tubes enveloping him.

We formed a small circle around his platoon sergeant, who was lying in a nearby bed and who despite his injuries raved about the bravery of his men. "I'm sorry I got wounded; I couldn't see the mission through," was the first thing he said when we all walked in. Colonel McMaster told him that he had done his duty and that we were all proud of him before presenting him the Purple Heart Medal. I led us in a quiet prayer for Smith and the others who had been injured and killed. We stayed 30 more minutes in the busy hospital, then flew back to Camp Sykes.

When I conducted the critical incident debriefing a few days later the driver of the tank was the most upset. He wasn't injured, but his guilt was devouring him and he sobbed as he contemplated starting over with a new crew. I tried to appear objective and calm as I listened to the soldiers talk about the incident, but I was beginning to twitch with anger at the endless carnage. The chapel's small heater struggled to pump air all around us. It felt like we could have drowned in there and no one would have been ordered to save us.

I thought of a newspaper ad that Ernest Shackleton had published ahead of his ill-fated 1907 *Endurance* expedition to the South Pole: "Men wanted for hazardous journey, Small wages, Bitter cold, long months of complete darkness, constant danger, safe return doubtful. *Honour and recognition in case of success . . .*" We were all on an endurance expedition with small pay, harsh weather, and safe return hardly guaranteed. Would there be honor and recognition in case of success?

Early November 2005
I have quite a responsibility to raise my two boys. When I get back, how will I fare? I keep waiting for the chaos outside to interrupt me. I am ready to go home and let my guard down. It will be nice to be in Bekah's arms and feel her touch. I miss her beautiful brown eyes.

I'm still working up the courage to just be. I have always valued security but what I have lacked is the fortitude to be my own person. I am consistently on edge these days and this is not good.

I was sending out prayer requests as often as I could, but I was also receiving them. My closest friend, Geoff Bailey, with whom I first studied to be an army chaplain back in 2000, had e-mailed me asking, "Could you please pray for our soldiers as well?" He was counseling soldiers stationed in Korea who hadn't had a day off in two months. Many had already been in Iraq and were about to deploy again. He said, "As a result, they will have no downtime and we are really starting to see a lot of increases in domestic issues, alcoholism, etc. I keep making recommendations and getting ignored as the incidents increase. The soldiers who deployed are also showing symptoms of PTSD but the train is moving too fast to take care of them."

I prayed for him right away, afraid I'd forget as the speeding train of my own deployment once again stole my attention. I asked God to watch over him, his men, and his chain-of-command. Later I wrote back to him to tell him how I was faring, and how I wasn't allowing myself to be pushed around anymore either, a problem we loved to commiserate over.

Bro,

A funny story for you: I went to the chow hall with a friend in my PT uniform several Sundays ago. Well, the guards at the entrance said that we had to have our weapons in order to enter. When I told the guard that I was a chaplain and I don't carry a weapon, you could see his bewildered expression. He turned to the other guard and said stumbling through his sentence, "Well, I guess you can go back and change in to your DCUs and come back." I looked at him (like he was stupid) and said, "I am not playing this game. Go ahead and take down my name; I'm going in." He followed me in and told the sergeant major and it was straightened out.

So my new statement when I disagree with something is, "I am not playing this game." What do you think?

Rebekah and the boys are in Austin visiting family. They are doing well. I'm a traveling man these days as I travel about 4 days a week in Tal Afar visiting my guys. It is nice and time seems to go faster. I'm preaching about 3 times a week.

Will be glad to get back home and normalize. These last three years have been fast and furious.

Talk to you soon,

Roger

▲▲▲

Early December 2005

I've been working this morning on fellowship game ideas for our Christmas party. Seng should be back from Mosul today, he has strep throat. I'm listening to Christmas music and I miss my family, it is so much harder around the holidays. I want to get Bekah something really nice since she has sacrificed so much.

I need to move closer to God. I don't want to go back angry and bitter. The other day I went into the Moral, Welfare & Recreation Center and it was so loud and crowded. I called Rebekah and the whole time my anxiety was building. I am not used to being around large groups of people. I had to leave the center—it was the only thing I could focus on. I ran into a couple of people from my unit and I guess they could see the expression on my face and they asked if everything was all right. My nerves are shot.

My conversation with Bekah had been tense from the start. I was forced to wait in line for the phone in the crowded center as soldiers played pool, came in and out of a small gym, and milled about talking. The noise in the hall took me by surprise since it usually wasn't so crowded. By the time I was able to call Bekah I could only talk for 5 minutes before I had to get off the phone and out of that hall.

I had been going outside the wire half of every week, but when I was back on the base I was becoming something of a hermit. I would eat and then hide out in my room, visiting less often with the guys on the base. Now, standing there in that recreation room after being in combat outposts all week, I felt overwhelmed with the noise and freedom of movement of those around me. The scene around me started to fade and fuzz over, and all I could see was a hot flash of anxiety that seemed to be shooting from my eyes. I fled.

I rushed back to the chapel and locked the door. I lay on the couch for about 10 minutes with my eyes closed, played some classical music on my computer, and wrote in my journal. I told myself I'd be fine. Yet as the week progressed, all I wanted, increasingly, was just to be left alone.

A few days later I tried calling Bekah again. As a pastor, I understood that coming home from deployment could be a tricky time for families. I didn't want to advise other soldiers what to do and not do it myself, so we had a long talk about our expectations before living with each other again. She once told me that she loved that about me—that I took our marriage seriously and worked on it with creativity and pleasure. She wanted us to prioritize dinners together as a family. I also wanted quality family time, including time on my own with the boys so they'd get to know me again. But I also needed time alone to adjust to being back. We worked out a plan to swap babysitting to help each other maintain our sanity. She'd watch them for an hour while I ran; I'd watch them for an hour while she did whatever she wanted. We had it all figured out.

10

▲▲▲

4 8 H O U R S

New Year's Eve 2005
Last day of the year and I am ready to end it. I feel that it
has been a good year of ministry. For the most part, I have
trusted the Lord to guide me through the days. It has been
rough though, I have gone through the depths of pain and
despair over the course of this deployment. This certainly has
been a trying time and the fact that I made it through this
is a testimony to God's goodness! I feel as if I can do anything
after this second combat tour.

I WAS EXCITED to go home in a few days but I also felt
guilty. I had been chosen to run the entire reintegration program for our regiment as it returned home, so I'd
be leaving one month early to set up for them. It was a
huge responsibility and an honor. But it also meant that
my squadron would have to work with another chaplain
they weren't as familiar with during their final days in
Iraq. I dreaded coming home only to get another e-mail

about another soldier like Brady. Seng would stay behind to assist the new chaplain until the regiment returned home, but it still felt wrong. I hated to leave them.

Two days—forty-eight hours. That was all the time I had left in Iraq. After some scrambled eggs and toast at the mess hall, I made my rounds on camp, visiting soldiers before they convoyed out and praying with those who asked for it. I was genuinely sorry to be leaving. Life may have been difficult and precarious there, but it was also distilled to the very basics. There were no distractions. There wasn't even time to mourn death. We followed orders, had no use for money, were fed on schedule, and our clothes were washed for us. As for me, if I did my job right, all I needed was to focus on God and on the soldiers.

I headed back to my office to make a thermos of Starbucks and then strolled over to the Lion Battery tactical operations center. It had rained overnight and the usually dry air now smelled crisp and earthy. A lieutenant was standing at the ink board with a marker poised in his hand. The radio chatter was cranked up high.

"What's going on?' I asked.

"A Blackhawk is missing." He went on. "Last night two helicopters were en route here from Mosul and when the lead helicopter landed, the other one was missing. Weather. We're out there looking for it now."

"Do we know who was on it?" I asked.

"No. But there were twelve on board. And there might have been some of our people on that bird." "Bird" was Army talk for helicopter.

We anxiously awaited the news and by noon they

had found the wreckage. Perhaps the flight crew had accidentally flown too low, but we'd never know for certain. Ten soldiers, three from our regimental staff, and two contractors were on board. One of the soldiers was a devout Catholic who helped lead services at our camp, another was a lieutenant who had recently pulled me aside to ask me to pay special attention to one of his soldiers who he worried wasn't faring well psychologically.

I remembered how, during my first deployment, half a dozen helicopters had gone down. One was shot down over Fallujah. A soldier I counseled described the frantic search for survivors and screams coming from the wreckage. Dead in that crash was another young soldier I knew, Sgt. Ron Hagerty. His mother had just died; a few hours before the crash we had prayed together for her before scrambling him on the first bird out so he could make it home for her funeral. I could only imagine the sorrow of his father; losing a wife and a son in the same weekend.

Dutifully, I took my place in the assembly line. Six five-ton trucks carrying the bodies idled nearby, as did dozens of soldiers we had enlisted as pallbearers for the Hero Flight. I must have stood in formation for nearly an hour as they unloaded the flag-draped caskets from the trucks and loaded them onto the waiting C130 aircraft. In our formation I caught a glimpse of one of our captains, who just a few months earlier had talked one of the victims into coming to Iraq. Guilt coated his face as the caskets were carried past him. The wind was blowing hard. In 24 hours these bodies would be back in Colorado and I'd be following right behind them.

Early January 2006
We lost a 101st bird early this morning and three of the
Regimental staff were killed in the crash. All three were
married and had kids. With only a month to go, they will
not return home. Makes me think of a question that has
been in my mind for quite a while. Did they know it was the
last minutes of their lives? So many have died over the last
two deployments, and I have not grieved properly. I was just
on a helicopter the other day. I feel as I have been altered
from my experiences in Iraq. It is a queer sense that I cannot
shake.

Part Two

▲▲▲

H O M E

11

▲▲▲

RUNNER'S HIGH

Kuwait, Mid-January
We're in Kuwait and our plane should take off at 2:20 a.m.
This is very disorienting as I'll be home super-fast compared
to OIF1 [first deployment] where we had two weeks to men-
tally prepare. I have to keep reminding myself that I'm
going home and not coming back here.

IRAQ HAD FELT like a giant race I hoped to survive, but now, safely back on U.S. soil, I couldn't stop running.

Fort Carson is surrounded by jogging trails, and I looped them endlessly like a caged animal on a wheel. One morning after an hour on the trail, I realized that the only sound for miles was my breathing and the soft thud of my sneakers as they hit the ground for a second before flying forward, ever faster uphill. Where was this energy coming from? At more than 6,000 feet, the air was thin and ice cold but I didn't seem to need oxygen. They say it takes up to six weeks to adjust to the Colorado Springs elevation, but I needed no adjustment time. As soon as my boots hit the ground I was home, and I was running.

In the distance, Cheyenne Mountain came into view, looming over Fort Carson like a guardian spirit. I couldn't remember ever seeing mountains so beautiful. I ran even faster, cutting through the cold wind with what felt like aerodynamic lightness. It was here that I finally achieved what I could never capture in Iraq: a clear view. With it was a new perspective on God's ultimate creation: life. I loved life. My lungs full of clean, crisp air, I looked into the sky and silently thanked God for the air and for the grass so green it looked painted by angels. Thank you, I said, for the chance to run. Thank you that, after two deployments, I still have my two legs and two feet to propel me ever faster. Thank you for teaching me that life is precious and we don't have a second to waste.

I turned at a bend in the trail. This time I was running for home.

As the trail looped around the base I ran past our residential area dotted with the town homes of my fellow Third Armored Cavalry officers. To an Iraqi they'd appear identical, just as the sand-drab homes of Tal Afar had looked to me.

I slowed down as I turned the corner of our street and reached the front of 7810B Light Fighter Drive, a blue, two-story townhouse like all the others. I bounded up the steps and unlatched the door, which I had left unlocked. What a relief not to worry about security. Tyler was at school and I could hear Bekah and Blaine eating breakfast in the kitchen. Everyone was safe.

▲▲▲

IT WAS HARD to realize I was truly home. Just two days earlier I had touched down on U.S. soil, as always keeping my journal close at hand.

> I was able to talk with a WWII Veteran that greeted us at the airport. He helped liberate the Jews from the concentration camps and he described their joy of being liberated. It must have been quite an experience and I have the most respect for him and the other WWII Vets. I do not feel the same about what I have done but maybe I will feel different years from now.

I was of two minds. In Iraq I felt like I was on the cutting edge of history. We were helping the local populace free themselves of Iraqis who used atrocities like beheadings and kidnappings to gain the upper hand. Yet on a larger scale I didn't feel I was coming home with a clear moral victory, like the World War II vet who freed the concentration camp victims. What I did know during those first hours in the United States was that

> in 16 hours, I will be with Bekah and that brings a smile to my face.

I wanted to be home and never leave again.
I arrived in Colorado in the middle of the night with

about fifty other soldiers, the first group to return from our unit. It was 1:00 a.m. when we filed into Waller gym for the greeting ceremony. We were in formation for about 15 minutes, and despite the 72 hours of travel, none of us were bleary-eyed. We were all desperate to run to our families, watching us from the bleachers across the gym floor, just within our grasp. When the soldier at the microphone said the magic words, "Now, go find your families," the passionate chaos, the teeming mass hug, began. Collective relief swept through the room as mothers, wives, husbands, and children were able to touch their soldiers, to hear their voices, finally home, alive and well, together.

Bekah practically tackled me with the biggest hug her 5-foot-2-inch frame could rally. The boys were sleeping at a friend's house that night. The plan was that we'd have time alone, with the added benefit that the boys wouldn't be cranky the next day, our first day together in a year without a looming return to Iraq. As soon as I walked into the door of my house, I felt 40 pounds lighter, the fear and the exhaustion just vanished.

Our first few days were a blissful mix of a second honeymoon and a very special Christmas. It was late January but we still had a tree, the latest stop-loss victim at Fort Carson, extended way past tour of duty. As everyone else was driving to work that January morning, we opened presents and sang carols. Months earlier I had sent home desert-camouflaged backpacks for the boys—Tyler's with Spiderman and Blaine's with Blue from *Blue's Clues*. For Bekah I had various gifts, including a brown Iraqi silk dress and a gold necklace. But I had been absent so long that the rest of the presents under the tree were a surprise to me. Blaine got a Rock 'N' Jazz Guitar and Tyler, a Playmobil pirate ship. I was supposed to be one of two adults in the room, but I was as excited as the boys to see what Mom and Dad had gotten them for Christmas.

▲▲▲

FOR THE NEXT two months, as the rest of our soldiers returned home, I was tasked with leading the regiment's reintegration program. This was a huge logistical challenge but, luckily, logistics were my forte (knowing how to avoid snipers was not). We had all seen the poor job our regiment had done of welcoming us back from our first tours—the Brady Westins who slipped through the cracks, the nearly two out of ten U.S. troops who returned home with depression, anxiety, or PTSD. This time we all wanted it to be different.

We had a $250,000 budget and about a dozen conference and ballrooms booked at the local Windham Hotel for what we'd call the Veteran's University. Every returning soldier would be offered a battery of seminars—on combat stress, marriage enrichment, money management, and communicating with children. We'd cycle in more than fifty instructors to teach the courses. There was even a seminar for singles and one for the recently divorced. I was in charge of everything from curriculum to table size for the thousands of soldiers and spouses who would go through the seminars. For ten months, I had longed for quiet time with my family, but my days were disappearing into the windowless ballrooms of the Windham Hotel. My mind was obsessed only with the questions facing soldiers: Does my family still need me? Why are the kids ignoring me? As for the spouses, I wanted them to know their concerns would be answered too: Did I do okay with the kids? Will I have to stop seeing my friends so much? Do we still have things to talk about?

The most important family advice for soldiers was simple: Don't try to whip things into shape overnight. Take time to learn how your family has changed while you were gone. Resist the temptation to go on shopping splurges.

There were, of course, more complex issues that wouldn't be so easy to address. I was most concerned about the soldiers coming home with combat stress. Our instructors warned them to keep an eye out for common problems: emotional distance with loved ones, withdrawal, nightmares, startled reactions, alcohol or drug abuse. Before I left Iraq, Maria had shown me a CNN video that recounted the experiences of vets; she used it in her reintegration classes back at Fort Hood. I liked its message: Everyone's trauma is unique and we all respond differently to war.

Soldiers needed to be aware of the symptoms of combat stress, and their leaders needed to keep an eye on them and quickly refer them for help. The problem was that getting or giving help wasn't so simple: Many of the leaders had combat stress themselves and, to make matters worse, our Fort Carson mental-health department was understaffed. This was a one-shot deal for us to be sure the soldiers had a chance to accept and explore what they'd been through, not sweep it under the rug.

The reintegration program was stressful, and the hours were long. The first few weeks I was home by six every night for dinner, but as the program went into action there were many nights when I missed the family meal despite my pact with Bekah. In order to make up for the lost family time, Bekah started bringing Blaine to the hotel to have lunch with me. That's the paradox of war; we know when we're going down the wrong path by not taking care of our personal needs, but the relentless urgency of our work makes it easiest to put our mission first, and our personal lives second. At that moment my mission was to ensure that more than four thousand soldiers and seven hundred spouses would have the safest, healthiest homecoming the Army could give them. I figured Bekah and I were strong enough and that our needs as one small family could wait just a little bit longer.

Mid-February 2006
Yesterday, after coming from the dry cleaners, a sergeant major corrected me for walking while Retreat was sounding. I went off on him. I was so angry and all the anger & frustration from home and work came out. Today Bekah and me are bumping heads. I don't like the way she's talking to me. We are both distant and frustrated with each other. What is wrong with me?

Sifting through hundreds of pages of presentations and hours of video footage about how deployments can strain relationships made it hard for me to believe the growing stress between Bekah and me was unique. We were like pieces of a puzzle that had been left out too long in the rain—we were bigger than before, expanded with experience and frayed at our edges—but we were still designed to fit together.

I counseled soldiers not to rush to take charge of discipline, routines, or finances at home, yet I had a hard time holding back myself. When I did jump in, reciting a bedtime story instead of reading one, or giving the boys a bath right after dinner instead of just before bed, Tyler would shout, "Mommy, Daddy does things wrong." I was no longer sure of what the rules or routines were. Bekah did her best to give me educational tips—after lunch we play for thirty minutes and *then* have a nap—but I had a hard time remembering all the new information and as the weeks progressed just backed off.

I had known I would need some time alone to readjust, but I needed much more than I ever had imagined. I also needed distance—miles in front of me that I could run through and conquer, not the four walls of a town home that sometimes felt like an upholstered cage. It wasn't that I didn't want to be with my family, it was just that our home wasn't big enough when I couldn't sit still. When Bekah and I watched TV at night, I would try to burn off my energy by doing sit-ups and push-ups.

"You're driving me crazy, sweetie," she would say from her cozy perch on the couch.

"Just a few more, hon." Then I'd do two hundred.

She was less patient about my weight loss and worried that I was damaging my health by losing too much. It was unusual for me to skip meals, but suddenly I wasn't hungry. I felt light and happier. By dieting—eating mostly Special K and oatmeal—I was ridding myself of the excess baggage left over from the generous care packages sent to Iraq. By running, I was getting rid of the excess energy. I moved from the trails to running a 5-mile course through the Garden of the Gods—a dramatic stretch of giant rock formations. Bekah complimented me when I had dropped 15 pounds but got worried when after two months I had lost nearly 30.

Then there were the nightmares, the ones that woke me up with a racing heartbeat and dragged Bekah out of her slumber. I couldn't figure it out. I had never been in a vehicle that was blown up, never been hit by a bullet— why was I dreaming about those things? I had prayed over bodies and heard more stories of bloodshed than I could recount, but had only faced a fraction of the danger that most soldiers had. So what was my problem? I knew that nightmares were a potential sign of PTSD. I can't say I had written the book on PTSD, but I *had* written the PowerPoint presentation. The signs were surfacing. I wasn't terribly worried though; most of the time I felt euphoric, not depressed. When I started to feel deflated, I would run, and that would fill me back up again.

Bekah thought that one way to cheer me up and for us to bond as a family would be to explore new churches together. We'd be moving to Washington, D.C., soon for my army hospital residency—I had been accepted at Walter Reed Army Medical Center—and we'd no longer be living on a military base. So it would be a good idea, she figured, to find an alternative to the on-post chapels we had grown used to and to try New Life Church, a megachurch that met for Saturday and Sunday services for up to five thousand people at a time.

As soon as we arrived, I realized I couldn't handle it. After having been in Iraq, its giant, 15-foot-high stadium-style entrances felt more like a coliseum to me than a place of worship. We had child care booked for the boys, but Tyler was on one side of the church and Blaine on another. There were so many children that the rooms were split up by month: 24-month-olds born between February and May would go to one room, June through September to another, and so on. We had to divide and conquer, with Bekah taking Tyler so she could explain his diabetes needs, while I took Blaine to his playroom. When we met again, I was disoriented. The pastor spoke from a stage in the center of the packed hall, surrounded on all sides by the word *Calibrate* scrawled across giant electronic screens. I couldn't focus. Thankfully the lights soon dimmed and we all started singing. It was beautiful in its own modern, high-tech way. But I still felt more moved by my soldiers singing in the dusty, makeshift chapel of Camp Sykes.

The calm didn't last long enough. At the end of the service the church descended into mass chaos with thousands of people streaming toward food stands or their cars as if they were leaving a baseball game, not a spiritual sanctuary. I had been to megachurches before and had been moved by the adrenaline and fellowship of the crowd; now it felt threatening.

"I'll get Blaine and then let's split," I suggested to

Bekah, who raced off for Tyler. But when I came back with Blaine to our appointed spot, she and Tyler were standing in what seemed like an endless line for cotton candy.

"We need to leave now, honey; this is a madhouse." She didn't budge. I really wanted to go. I had been extremely uncomfortable from the moment we entered the church. Now the stirring dread in my gut told me I *had* to leave.

"We'll be ready in a sec," she told me.

And that's when a burning white light of rage passed in front of my eyes, nearly blinding me with its intensity.

"No, we need to go, now," I said it as slowly and calmly as I could muster.

"Roger, his blood sugar is low. We *need* a snack, now. Just go out to the car and we'll meet you there." There were so many people moving around us that it was hard to breathe. The crowd seemed to be pushing and shoving now.

"It's not safe."

"*What?*"

"It's not safe . . . to go out to the car, alone." Bekah looked at me as if I had just sprouted horns from my head but stepped away from the line. Tyler had the first looks of fury on his face as we all walked together to the car. We picked up some French fries from McDonald's on the way home. Bekah ordered a soda—half diet, half regular—so Tyler would get some fast sugar.

Bekah agreed the church was too crowded but she didn't understand why I couldn't wait in the car while she fed Tyler. She didn't understand that I couldn't let us split up amid that chaos.

It just wouldn't have been safe.

▲▲▲

I WAS WALKING on post one day between counselings when Chaplain Bixler pulled me aside. "Stop by and see me," was all he said.

Bixler, an important mentor in my life, was in his sixties, with a gentle spirit and a voice so quiet I often asked him to repeat himself. I went right over to his house, where he had converted his basement into a cozy office.

Bixler and I had counseled Brady Westin together and he let me ramble about him for a while. As a family-life chaplain, Bixler worked a tremendous amount with Brady while at Fort Carson and was as torn up by his death as I was. But the conversation meandered and it soon became clear that Bixler wanted to talk about me. He had counseled me after my first deployment and knew I was sensitive to the deaths of soldiers. Bixler also had strong views about the Army's care of chaplains, or lack thereof. He told me he was counseling several chaplains, that so often they were left out in the cold. "I'm not sure what it is that people assume," he mused. "Maybe that God will take care of us, or that we should know how to take care of ourselves. It makes people uncomfortable if a chaplain isn't feeling well." I sat silently as he described the signs of PTSD he saw emerging in me—that I was apparently speaking in a monotone and had a distant look to my eyes.

"Who are you angry with?" he asked. I told him I was angry with myself for letting my soldiers down, especially when I was away on leave, and now for leaving them early again for the re-integration program. I told him about an e-mail Maria sent me soon after I arrived here. She had traveled outside the wire with Chaplain Causey and Seng to visit Grim Troop at their Forward Operating Base in Tal Afar. Within a minute of their arrival, some dismounted soldiers were hit by an IED. She wrote that she had seen the whole event, from blast to MEDEVAC to the detainment of possible suspects. "It was quite an event to witness," she wrote, "but it made things more real. To see U.S. soldiers wounded and bleeding was just too much, but Causey was a trooper. He jumped into action and before you knew it, he was part of a litter team." That meant he was carrying our soldiers on stretchers while I was hanging out in a four-star hotel. It was once again hard to understand which of my worlds was the real one: Tal Afar or Colorado Springs. At times they both felt like fiction.

"It's important to understand your expectations and your limitations," Bixler advised. "Why don't you ask yourself this: What would Brady Westin tell you to do? Do you think he blames you for his death? Just think about it, think by yourself." Bixler wasn't a fan of group therapy or combat stress debriefings. He hated the Army's approach to healing, and thought all it did was re-traumatize people with others' trauma. He knew that within a month I'd be leaving Fort Carson for my new chaplain training at Walter Reed, and was worried I might not be psychologically prepared for it.

"Are you praying?" he asked. "Are you talking with God about your anger?"

Now I was beginning to get annoyed with this soft-spoken inquisition.

"Yes, maybe." I didn't really want to talk. Lately when I prayed, my mind would stray to the faces of the soldiers we'd lost over our two deployments—including Brady; Hagerty, who had died en route to his mother's funeral; or Private Byrd, whom I counseled before he died of pneumonia. I wasn't angry with God. I just found it harder to think clearly about Him when other faces competed with his image

"Why don't you talk with God about your feelings?" he suggested.

I said I would, but I wasn't sure I could.

I knew he was right, but I just wanted to get home, where Bekah was impatiently waiting for me for dinner. I prayed he wouldn't press me further, and he didn't. He let me go, but not without a promise to come back.

Mid-February 2006

I met with CH Bixler yesterday. I guess I am mad at my-self because I felt that with my knowledge, position, and experience—I shouldn't be having these problems. I feel as if I'm weak-minded and am disappointed in myself. I also know that I'm extremely stressed by the reintegration pro-gram. I know that I discount my struggles and that plays into me taking too much on. I'll continue to see CH Bixler on a weekly basis because I think a lot of my issues stem from unresolved grief over combat losses.

It was a shock to the system when the reintegration program was over. Don't get me wrong; after two solid months of planning, prepping, and execution, I was ready for a break. We had trained thousands of soldiers in the art of coming home gracefully and safely. Whether or not they would take advantage of their newfound knowledge, I didn't know, but we had done our best and I was proud to be part of such a program. My next mission? To go on block leave, a period where everyone in the regiment is on orders to relax.

We camped out for a week in Bekah's parents RV in an Austin state park. I ran countless miles every morning and played with the kids in the afternoons. After that Bekah and I had struck gold—we had a free stay on a seven-day Caribbean cruise because they needed a chaplain to conduct a religious service. Those weeks were a nice break, a fuzzy blur like all vacations are. I remember mountains and parks and blue oceans but mostly that Bekah and I were the happiest we'd been in a long time. I could jog on the ship's oval running track and take in the majesty of the sea; she could read a book in peace for the first time in more than a year. Each night we dressed up and ate dinner together in the ship's elegant dining rooms, laughing as we snapped photos of the food. The presentation was so amazing and over-the-top that we had to show the boys later. Bekah got every "cure" imaginable: manicure, pedicure; I teased her that she was wholly cured.

Bekah and I led the service as a team. We hadn't done any form of ministry together since college when we helped others conduct services. Now we were leaders. I welcomed the passengers and then passed the baton to Bekah, who led a song worship before I started the formal sermon. We had eighty passengers in attendance and they requested two more services. We had only been scheduled for one, but we were more than happy to do more.

Even the crew asked for a service. They were mostly Philippino, working hard to send money back to their families at home. Bekah had a long conversation with one crew member who had a boy Blaine's age but had to live apart from him in order to provide for her family. The crew reminded us how lucky we were as Americans, how much we had compared to so many families across the world. They were so busy working that the only time we could schedule a service for all forty of them was at midnight. The night of the service we crawled into bed just before ten, curled up together, and woke up to an alarm two hours later. If we were tired we quickly forgot it as soon as we began the service. Their spirituality, the way that they sang and prayed and listened, was the best memory of our trip. We both returned home feeling that God would continue to use us in ministry.

▲▲▲

MY TIME AT Fort Carson was coming to an end. It was late May 2006 when I sat down with Lieutenant Colonel Hickey to receive my yearly Officer Evaluation Report (OER), my official report card for the year. I had spent thirty-five months in extreme conditions either training to deploy or being deployed. The time had transformed me, I thought, from a naïve young guy with no under-standing of the horrors of war to an experienced captain and chaplain. During that ten months in Tal Afar I had conducted more than three hundred counseling sessions, twenty-four Critical Incident Stress Debriefings, sixty Protestant services, seven memorial ceremonies for eight soldiers and had been outside the wire dozens of times to visit the soldiers in Tal Afar. I couldn't believe I would now be leaving Sabre Squadron, the soldiers who had be-come my second family.

"We did it," said Hickey, holding my evaluation in his hand. This was a guy who epitomized the meaning of the word *integrity*. If he said it, I took his word. We had fin-ished our tour in Tal Afar, he told me, and we made a real difference. We remembered how when we first arrived the schools were closed, kids didn't dare to walk the streets, and their parents paid dearly for cooperating with Coalition forces. We recalled one traffic circle where in-surgents had left decapitated bodies, their severed heads perched on the bodies as a warning not to deal with U.S. troops. But in recent months people had once again filled the streets. The Iraqi Army was becoming more profi-cient, local government was functioning, and Iraqis had come out in droves to vote in the December national elections. As we sat in that room, hundreds of patients were cycling safely through the hospital where snipers had shot at us, receiving medical care they couldn't get before we arrived. All the training, the endless hours, the uncomfortable environment—as I talked with Hickey I realized it was all worth it. I had earned a Combat Action

Badge, two Bronze Stars and two Army Commendation Medals, but one of my greatest rewards was hearing Hickey say we had done our job well, and that we had done it together.

Hickey handed me my report.

"Chaplain (Captain) Roger Benimoff continues to prove that he has a great future in the Army Chaplaincy." It noted my selection as the regimental reintegration officer for our 4,500 returning soldiers and how "Roger's valuable out-of-the-box thinking and eighteen months of combat experience were instrumental in building the training curriculum from the ground up . . . since then Roger has expertly provided pastoral care to our wounded Soldiers and counseled others in the areas of marriage, work, and spiritual matters." I could only glance at some of the other phrases, "promote ahead of peers" and "Benimoff is a must select for promotion to Major." At that moment I had no doubt I had found my life's calling.

Bekah and I celebrated that night. So much was ahead of us and we were so excited to see Washington D.C. We would go on trips to all the monuments, get to know this country I served. After three years we would finally be a family again.

12

▲▲▲

WALTER REED

Rebekah Benimoff, Early July 2006
Philippians 4:6
"Do not be anxious about anything, but in everything, by
prayer and petitions, with thanksgiving present your re-
quests to God."

I don't know how to deal with Roger. Moving seemed to
set off some deep-seated anger in him, and he is difficult to
be around and even harder to talk to. He cannot answer
simple questions. . . . I ask him "Do you want a sandwich?"
and his answer is so often "I can't talk about that right
now." I cannot plan what we'll do on the weekend because
he can't discuss it. This drives me crazy. I want to plan
something—do something to keep the kids occupied until
school starts. Even if we just go to a nearby park.

NEITHER OF US knew what to expect in our new life, and
tensions were quickly running high. We had driven out

east and rented a home in Silver Spring, Maryland. The boys were a handful for Bekah as she unpacked and sorted out school issues concerning Tyler's diabetes care. I, meanwhile, tried to keep my head above water during my first weeks at Walter Reed.

Walking the campus, I realized how far I had come from my fuel specialist days and couldn't believe I had made it here. The Walter Reed Army Medical Center, opened in 1909, has treated veterans from World War I to Vietnam to Iraq. The campus, 113 acres of rolling lawns and red brick buildings, is devoted to helping soldiers recover from the horrors of war and is considered by many to be the premier symbol of medical care for American soldiers. I was thrilled to be a part of it. Not only would I have a long break from combat, but my one-year assignment here would qualify me to pastor inside army hospitals. I would also counsel outpatients and, outside of the program, work toward a Doctorate in Ministry degree.

In the mornings my residency class of nine chaplains trained and critiqued one another; in the afternoons we counseled patients. The director of the program, Chaplain David O'Connor, never tired of reminding us that our job was to examine our own existence, and not just get caught up in daily routines. We should focus on "being," not just "doing." It was tough work. It helped that I was among friends: One of the other chaplains was Geoff Bailey, who had been one of the most supportive voices in my prayer group while in Iraq. Every month we worked several 24-hour shifts, and I was one of two chaplains assigned to the Psych Ward's stabilization unit, where returning soldiers with profound mental-health problems were housed.

The Psych Ward was tightly secured. Each time I was buzzed in, a heavy metal door clicked behind me, a sound that never ceased to make me anxious. The ward housed about two dozen patients. Some were older and past active duty but most were in their early twenties, either fresh from Iraq, or sent to Walter Reed from different U.S. forts that couldn't handle severe disorders like schizophrenia.

The patients' routines were tightly controlled: On their ink-board schedule for each day was a 30-minute bloc for "SPIRITUAL UPLIFTING." That meant me. I was accustomed to waiting for soldiers to ask me for advice, but these patients wouldn't talk unless I approached them first. This was my first time working with people with profound mental-health disorders, which unnerved me, especially since I was given so little time to allow these men and women to warm to my presence on the ward. I tried to engage the patients by asking if it was okay to sit with them. Most said yes.

My groups varied in size, but usually about five to ten patients would pull up chairs in a U-shaped circle to meet with me. During these sessions, as in Iraq, I often worked from notes taken from *The Purpose Driven Life*, broken down very simply with the aim to have the patients reflect on what they wanted out of their own lives. We talked about putting our trust in finite things like people, material wealth, careers, and success, and how easy it was to be disappointed by them. If we build our lives on a solid foundation such as our faith, I told them, we could handle the trials of life that bombard us on a daily basis. But if we build our lives upon sand, we will surely crumble.

After each session I would hang around in case anyone on the ward wanted to talk. We were not allowed to psychoanalyze patients—we weren't trained for that. But we were there to hear their sacred stories if and when they wanted to share them. Surprisingly, most patients were willing to open up, and I found this spiritually uplifting as it was hard for me to share my own feelings lately; each day seemed like a struggle for me too.

Because this was a stabilization unit, nobody stayed for long, and every few days there were new faces to familiarize myself with. One day one of the ward techs pointed me toward a patient who had just arrived, Camila, who was Hispanic, in her mid-thirties, and suffering from severe panic attacks after several Iraq deployments. I thought I'd just introduce myself so she knew she could come to me when she was ready. Then I'd move on to other patients I already knew. My plans changed as soon as Camila and I started to talk.

She was sitting with her back to me in a corner of the room, wearing a hospital gown and working on a puzzle. In one hand she held a puzzle piece; her other hand was bandaged.

"Camila?" She turned toward me and looked up. The room was noisy but she seemed subdued.

"I'm Chaplain Benimoff and I wanted to introduce myself to you."

"Okay."

"I'm here every day and I like to meet everyone and

see if I can serve them in any way. Are you working on a puzzle here?"

"Yeah, but there are pieces missing," she sounded disappointed. "I've tried to put it together but I can't."

"I bet that's frustrating."

"Yes!"

"Kind of like life . . . sometimes pieces of the puzzle are missing." It was a pretty simple thing to say and I said it lightly, so she could either take me seriously or brush it off. But she looked up into my eyes.

"It is."

"Do you want to talk"

She looked back down at her puzzle pieces and nodded yes.

"What brought you here?"

She began speaking softly, in short bursts.

"I've deployed to Iraq and Afghanistan five times and now I'm here. My husband did some bad stuff and I divorced him. I just want to be healed so I can be with my son."

"Camila, do you mind if I sit down?

"Not at all."

I sat and then leaned forward in my chair to make better eye contact.

"It's tough when all the pieces don't fit together," I repeated, looking at the puzzle but hoping she'd talk more about herself. "Is there anything you'd like to talk about? . . . When were you in Iraq?"

"Just a few months ago, I was blown up in my vehicle. Two of the soldiers with me were killed. I was thrown out of the Hummer with the soldier next to me, who lost his leg. We were lying there on the ground together. I remember kissing his hand. He was black and I think he kissed me back. I passed out and don't remember anything else."

As she spoke I briefly thought back to my time in Iraq and of Sergeant Miller's driver who had lost his leg.

Camila continued. "And people don't help."

"What do you mean?"

"People don't really care. It's like when you have a toy dinosaur but it's missing an arm or a leg. Nobody wants to play with it—they only want to play with the dinosaurs that have their arms and legs, the ones that still work."

Here was a woman who felt profoundly discarded, a feeling that ran rampant here. Yet she wanted to be cured. In John 5:7 there is an invalid at the pool at Bethesda who had been crippled for thirty-eight years. When Jesus asks him if he wants to be well, the invalid replies that he has no one to help him into the pool. But he didn't answer Jesus' question, "Do you want to get well?"

I wondered the same of myself. I wasn't well; I knew something was wrong, and I could tell my supervisors did too. But did I really want to get well? Part of me was proud to be a wounded healer because it helped me understand soldiers like Camila and it helped me better understand myself. The invalid had waited by that pool for thirty-eight years yet somehow didn't die of starvation. Someone must have been helping him. So Jesus' question strikes a little deeper: If the man is healed, he has to take responsibility for himself. That's not always so easy to do.

But in talking with Camila I pursued her metaphor, not mine. "You feel like the dinosaur with the one leg that has been discarded?"

"Yes. I just want to get better and be with my son."

"How old is he?"

"Sixteen."

"So, you want to be whole, to be healed so that can be with your child again?"

"Yes I do."

"How do you imagine that you can be whole so you can be with your son?"

"I don't know," she said, then shined an unexpected smile. "You know, I used to pray and go to church."

"Camila," I said, smiling too. "What is that smile all about?"

"I remember the first time my pastor preached. I had his sermons sent to me in Iraq."

I wanted to explore her smile a bit more.

"What stuck out about his sermons?"

"He talked about single mothers and how everyone makes mistakes. He talked about healing. I volunteered to be a prayer partner and I felt such a peace."

"Maybe that's a place to start?"

"Yeah, maybe . . . it's just been so long."

"If you were to pray to God, what would you say?" I asked.

She looked up and thought for a moment. "I would be thankful, I would thank God for saving my life. I remember being on the helicopter and seeing a light. I had a dream that I was flying and felt such a peace. I felt guided by God."

I took a stab in the dark here, wondering if she might feel any survivor's guilt.

"Have you been a little angry at God at the same time, maybe?"

"No, not really."

I was wrong, so I thought back to the start of our conversation. "So, maybe one of those puzzle pieces is reconnecting with God through prayer? To slowly heal and get your body and your mind healthy again . . . to become whole? Camila, would you like me to pray with you?

"Yes, I would."

"I have some sense of what you may want me to pray for, but do you have some specific ideas?"

"Salvation, wholeness . . . that I can be with my son."

We both bowed our heads. "Our God, we come to you and I want to lift up Camila. We pray that you would heal her physically and emotionally. We pray that you would make her whole and that she would be reunited with her son. We know you are with us and I pray that you would provide direction for Camila. It's in Jesus' name that we pray. . . . Amen."

When I looked up her face was peaceful.

"Thank you, Chaplain."

I stood up and we both smiled.

"You're most welcome."

Who is the healer and who is the patient, I wondered. In many ways I was a lot like Camila. I didn't see all the puzzle pieces and didn't feel entirely whole. But talking with her reminded me of the need to recall the times when I had experienced God's touch in my own life and to hold on to those moments with everything I had.

▲▲▲

By my second month I was engrossed in counseling—
and consumed by my own past. I told others to relax and
unwind, yet I couldn't take my own advice. I was surrounded by amputees and fresh combat casualties, re-
minders of the war I was trying to leave behind. All too
often, seeing them brought up memories of soldiers I had
known who were injured or killed.

Our training didn't help. They had us watch an HBO
documentary about medics in Baghdad, where the cam-
era crew followed ER teams through triage, amputations,
and visits to the morgue. The team filmed overwhelmed
and exhausted doctors, nurses, and chaplains. I was so
distraught from the footage that by the end of the video I
was sweating and nauseated. One of my chaplain peers
who had served in Iraq, Steve, said it had shaken him up
badly too. When I was called on to give my reaction, I
couldn't respond. Like so many soldiers in my debriefing
sessions in Tal Afar, I said I'd pass.

Certain patients on the psych ward affected me
deeply. There was one patient, Stephen, who had been
abused as a child and then sent to Iraq as an adult. His
story sent me into a downward spiral for days. Theodicy
is a branch of theology that attempts to reconcile the existence of evil or suffering with the belief in an omni-
scient, omnipotent, and benevolent God. The word itself
means "the justice of God" or, sometimes, "justification
of God." But theodicy could not help me reconcile the
question of Stephen as a boy: Why do bad things happen
to defenseless people? Since my primary task in this life

was serving God, I didn't like being left with such pivotal questions while ministering at the same time.

Stephen had what is known as Major Depressive Disorder, or MDD. During our talk in the group room, we had spoken about religion, and he said a strange thing: "I know I will be rewarded in heaven for all the things that were not my fault." He wore a blue hospital gown and smoked a cigarette. He told me how how his time in Iraq had compounded an already existing depression. He was only twenty-five and already looked much older.

Later, I wrote up notes from our talk.

> Theodicy. Why do bad things happen to defense-less people? This is what was going on in my mind as [S] talked. [S] talked about his childhood but I was scared to pursue it. There is always a question in my mind when I hear of this kind of injustice, why cannot God intervene in these instances and save the child the damage that the abuse will cause? It wouldn't seem to cost God too much to do this.
>
> According to the patient, part of the reason he is in his current situation is due to the abuse as a child. In the moment, I tried to reflect on specific themes or scriptures that might parallel his situation but none came to mind. Upon reflecting on the event, I think of 2 Samuel 13, where Amnon fell in love with Tamar, Absalom's sister. Amnon forces himself on Tamar, rapes her, and disgraces her. This makes me extremely angry and I celebrate when Absalom kills Amnon two years later.

Why is my response so strong? I believe this is partly due to being in situations where I had little control, such as in Iraq. Why couldn't God save all of us from having to witness and experience such senseless situations?

The problem lies in something even remotely bad being allowed to happen to those that are defenseless. Cognitively, I can reason this out. The human condition, free will, sinfulness, etc. all play a part in people being given the freedom to sin or not to sin. But emotionally, it hurts and causes a reaction within me. The feeling that hooks me is helplessness.

This raises a question that perplexes me: Why do some escape life's extreme vicissitudes and others seem to skate by? As a child of God, it would be logical to assume that God the Father would protect His children. However, this is not the case and not being protected by God makes me angry. As a father of a child, I would do everything within my means to protect my children. How can a good creator allow this kind of evil to exist?

I wanted to connect with the patient and it helped that we had several things in common. I did feel close to the patient and I could somewhat identify with his depression as I also suffer from it to a degree. Since I did feel like I connected with the patient, I talked longer than I normally would versus if I had gotten negative vibes. But I did get stuck in the latter part of the visit. At the time, I did not feel my anger. I mostly felt sad and my sadness was for him; not for me. Reflecting upon the visit, I realize that my sadness stems from my helplessness and sense of injustice in the world. I realize that I am angry at God for putting me in a helpless situation.

Each day my skills as a counselor eroded and I felt myself growing more and more similar to my patients. Though I had been worried about "differentiation" from the soldiers while in Iraq, here at Walter Reed I was slowly losing my self-discipline. All too often when patients confided in me I found it impossible to keep my own thoughts and feelings in check. While they spoke my mind kept wandering back to Iraq.

Lately I was arguing with everyone around me. There were days when I was angry from the moment I woke up, so, to avoid confrontation I began hiding from my family and my colleagues by keeping long hours in my office. I began seeing a psychiatrist, the tall and ever-calm Dr. William Lehman. Like me, he was a caregiver who had deployed to Iraq. He had experienced violence firsthand in the field and I felt comfortable talking to him about my nightmares, my plummeting weight, and my desire to throw myself into work, not family. To alleviate my swings between depression and hypervigilance, he prescribed me an array of medications for depression and nightmares, as well as Klonopin for anxiety and Trazodone for insomnia. We both knew this was a passing phase. Or so I thought.

We were finishing up a visit one morning in August when everything I thought about myself changed in a single minute. Lehman was reviewing my meds at his computer when I stood up and glanced at his screen. My eyes came to rest on his diagnosis of me, in bold print: "Chronic Post-Traumatic Stress Disorder." My heart sank. I sat back in the uncomfortable metal chair in a state of shock. I'd been trained in PTSD and its treatments, I'd taught combat stress classes, and led dozens of Critical Incident Stress Debriefings. How could I let this happen? The visit was almost over and I left as soon as I could, without saying a word about what I had seen.

Late August 2006
Physiologically my body is still reacting to perceived threats and I can hardly be in a noisy public place without having an anxiety reaction. There isn't a day that I don't think about some events from the war and many times sights, sounds, and other stimuli take me right back. I have good days and bad days. On my bad days sometimes it hurts so bad that I hurt physically. It is hard on Rebekah too. She is often embarrassed at my emotional outbursts. I am not motivated to work, I am not doing my readings and I don't care. The little minutia things about the Army don't interest me and I have lost a sense of my perfectionism in the process. I've been ruined. I worked so hard over the last three years that I have little will to do anything else. Nothing else seems to measure up to what we were able to accomplish in Iraq.

Bekah no longer asked me to come home for family dinners. Sometimes she would e-mail me psalms or marriage devotionals and I would send back sweet messages from work. I found that much easier than spending time with her in person, even if I knew she was lonely. Unlike our post in Colorado, there was no military community to welcome her and the boys to our new neighborhood, which made my long absences twice as hard on her. But at some point each night I would navigate the 9 miles to our house in Silver Spring, winding my way through the narrow roads and hoping my family would be asleep by the time I pulled into the driveway so I wouldn't have to face them.

One Saturday morning we woke up late. Looking forward to a quiet day at home I drank my coffee while watching the boys play in the yard. After being home alone all week, Bekah had a different plan for the day. She wanted us, as a family, to do some sightseeing. We had been near D.C. for more than a month and had yet to visit a single monument in the nation's capital. I thought we had already talked about this a few days earlier. I did not want to go anywhere that weekend, just hang out at home, and maybe do some catch-up work at my home office upstairs in the bedroom. In truth, I dreaded leaving the house.

"Let's go to the park up the street," I offered as a compromise. She turned on her heels and headed to the kitchen to get snacks for our trip, but was clearly angry. Soon after, as I drove to the playground Bekah wanted to have a talk, even though driving required all my energy. I was spending all my time at the office, she said; we had come here with the idea of exploring the area with the boys and now I was never around. She pressed me again and again on the same points. I held my ground, "We

should talk later." Everything was "later," she argued, and
so she kept at it. My head was spinning, my anxiety blinding me. That's when I completely lost it.

"Shut up! Just shut up and go away!" I shouted, repeating the same thing over and over and again, long
after Bekah had stopped talking.

She stared at me in horror. Perhaps I was yelling at
some unforeseen force, not her. Perhaps it would die
down. But I didn't stop, not for 10 minutes. I paid no
attention to the boys, who were thankfully engrossed in a
DVD in the backseat and wearing headphones.

Bekah finally struck back.

"Roger, you have been attacking me this whole
month. When you're not doing that, you're just neglect-
ing us. I'm not going to take this anymore."

"I haven't been attacking you, I haven't said a thing.
I've stayed out of your way. I've been totally quiet."

"You've called me a 'bitch,' Roger, and said that there
was no point in being married to a nag." Her words
stung, especially because Bekah never swore, and found it
hard to say that word now. I had been on a cornucopia of
medications, and didn't remember calling her names.

We stormed out of the car and I took the boys di-
rectly to the swings and began pushing them, as high and
as rough as they pleased. Bekah walked alone to the other
side of the playground. As she sat there crying, she resolved to take the boys with her to Austin, to her parents'
home. Not to get a divorce, but for a short separation.

Then she heard a voice telling her she had a choice:
You can walk away from your husband and your marriage

or you can be faithful. Let me heal him. Watching me swing the boys, she thought about what that voice inside her said, and answered that she was not strong enough to do that. The voice answered that she could walk in His strength, she didn't need to rely on herself. She vowed to try.

Rebekah Benimoff, Fall 2006
Feeling afraid to express any emotion around Roger as he just blows up. It does not matter what I am sharing—from a problem with the boys, or a question about the grocery list. He is simply impossible to deal with. It doesn't matter whether I am sharing negative feelings or positive ones. He interprets EVERYTHING as negative. I am at a loss. When I try to point out that I am being positive, he just gets angry. When I am frustrated about the kids he cuts me off and refuses to even discuss it. I need my husband to partner with me in raising our kids. I tend to be a perfectionist. He used to remind me to give them grace, and help me find solutions. Now he just yells at me and causes me more stress when I try to share my struggles. I know I am to stay in the marriage, but I have much trouble seeing any hope.

13

▲▲▲

SIDE EFFECTS

Early September
I have been back from Iraq for over 6½ months and am
having an extremely difficult time adjusting.

THE INSTITUTION OF marriage seemed to surround me
that fall. In September I flew to the Biltmore Estate in
Asheville, North Carolina, to officiate the wedding of
Cpt. Ryan Howell. Bekah and I were not getting along,
and she stayed home. I needed some time alone and I suspected she also could use a break from me.

My closest friends from Iraq would be there, especially those from Grim Troop, whom I had spent so
much time counseling outside the wire. I didn't agree to
do too many weddings because I required that couples
attend months of premarital counseling and most people didn't feel they could wait that long. Later they'd divorce on a whim. But when had Ryan asked me in Iraq to

officiate, I didn't think twice before saying yes. Over the course of our ten-month deployment, we had counseled more than enough, and even though I had not yet met Renee, his bride-to-be, I felt as if I already knew and liked her.

The first person I saw was First Sergeant Serrano. He had lost several soldiers from his troop—Brady had died in his arms—and I knew things had been tough for him as the deployment wrapped up. We were both spirited into the men's changing room to put on our dress blue uniforms. I was happy to see him, yet as Serrano and I dressed I realized I was growing anxious. I accepted a glass of wine and sat down on a cushioned chair. I reached into a pocket of the clothes I had just changed out of, which were lying in a heap at my feet, and pulled out a small pill case. I thought I was being surreptitious when I reached for my Klonopin, which acts like a time-release Valium, but Serrano noticed and quickly sat down next to me. I had no choice but to take a swig of wine to help me swallow the pill, right in front of him.

I was flushed with embarrassment.

"You know, I'm taking medication too."

First Sergeant Serrrano, on medication?

"Do you want to tell me about it?" I prodded. Here I was, always the master of asking questions but unable to share myself. He leaned in so none of the other seven or so guys in the room could hear us.

"Ambien because I can't sleep and Celexa for depression. They help me relax."

I was stunned. Even more than that, I was relieved.

"I've been having a hard time adapting," I told him. "When did you start taking the meds?"

"Two weeks after we got home, but I didn't want to tell anybody. I even tried some therapy. I couldn't sleep, I've been sick over Brady and the guys we lost. I've just got some anger problems, you know."

"I think I do too," I answered.

He told me he understood why I was upset. That I had to see everyone in all the squadrons, that I might counsel a thousand soldiers and never get counseling myself. My mind flashed to one night at that abandoned school when Captain Howell had asked me, "Chaplain, who's your chaplain?"

"You know," Serrano continued. "You were the only chaplain I'd ever talk to, maybe because you were a soldier first."

I realized that without knowing it, Serrano was counseling me.

"Thank you," was all I could respond.

"I didn't want to take any pills but the doctor told me I would be a good example to my soldiers. 'If you take care of yourself, they'll take care of themselves' was what he said. Nothing to be embarrassed about."

We both knew it wasn't quite as easy as that. I wanted to talk more but it was time to head outside for the big moment.

Soon I was surrounded by the same faces I had been in Iraq, but we were standing on acres of grass instead of patched sand, with one of the country's grandest estates looming behind us.

The crowd gathered—all the groomsmen in dress blues and the women in flowing pastel gowns. There were at least a hundred of them, and it was up to me to start the service. My words would be a mix of material from the United Methodist Book of Worship and a bit of humor, which I knew Howell would appreciate.

Friends, we are gathered here together in the sight of God to witness and bless the joining together of Ryan Howell and Renee Bussie in Christian marriage. The covenant of marriage was established by God, who created us male and female for each other. With His presence and power Jesus graced a wedding at Cana of Galilee, and in His sacrificial love gave us the example for the love of husband and wife.

With marriage not only comes the ups but also the downs. . . . How many present can attest to that? The truth is that marriage is a tough proposition. Some come to the conclusion that man was created to totally irritate the woman and many women wonder what creature has possessed the perfect man she once knew. What will keep two people together, who have totally different chemistries? What will keep a couple together when the honeymoon is over? When they have the house, the cars, and the 2.5 kids, the bills, and responsibilities? It is the Holy Covenant they established.

If the solemn vows you are about to make are kept faithfully, and if steadfastly you endeavor to do the will of your heavenly Father, your life will be full of joy, and the home you are establishing will abide in peace.

No other ties are more tender, no other vows more sacred than those you now assume.

Thrilled for the new couple, I pronounced Ryan and
Renee man and wife. I was relieved that the service went
well and now we could head toward dinner. I hadn't eaten
anything since before getting on the flight that morning.
As we waited to be served I chatted with a retired general
over several glasses of white wine. By the time the food
was served I was feeling a groggy mix of medication and
wine clouding my brain. All of the sudden my name was
called. I had forgotten that I would have to say the dinner
prayer. I stood up in surprise, walked several feet to the
center of the dance floor, and said a blessing for the food
and the occasion. I didn't quite slur my words, but they
didn't come easily either. When I sat back down and
everyone began to eat, I accepted glass after glass of
wine. I rarely drank, but at the moment alcohol was all I
wanted.

Sometime during the middle of dinner the faces surrounding me started to fall in and out of focus and my
stomach started to revolt. I excused myself from the table
and made it just ten feet into the hallway before I leaned
over and vomited against a wall. I hadn't realized that
Freddy had followed me out of the room. I felt his
hands pull me up by my armpits and drag me toward
the men's restroom. He helped me into a stall where I
continued to throw up as he made jokes to ease my
embarrassment. At one point he handed me a fancy
handkerchief. I wiped my mouth with it and then threw it
into the toilet. He laughed, "Chaplain, you weren't sup-

posed to flush that." The night continued downhill from there.

The next day I couldn't look anyone in the eye. I apologized to Freddy and the others, and the response from each was the same. "Don't worry, we're family."

Late September 2006, at airport headed home
I am very worried that I am not getting better.

   I cannot help to think about our KIAs. I just saw two soldiers in uniform here in the airport and automatically went to our killed. Hardly a day goes by when I don't think of memories or such. I feel like my mind is warped. I feel like there is a monster within me. Maybe I will go back and pay my dues.

   I am so down it is not funny. Even on the Valium and Celexa I am depressed. I wouldn't mind ending it all. The pain is unbearable. The wedding went well but even with the medicine I couldn't handle the anxiety of being with my Sabre family. I dread being with Bekah. I feel like an out-sider looking in on every area of my life. I wish I had died in Iraq. That would have been an honorable death. There were several chances and I am disappointed that I made it through. Rebekah would have got SGLI and USAA [life insurance]. Now I have to put up with this minutia and I hate being back. This does not measure up to what I've been through and yet what I've been through really sucked. What am I to do? I have to go home and pretend that every-thing is normal when I am dying inside. I work on the psych ward and I see the pitiful PTSD soldiers and I think I would just give up if I was to end up in there. I need my medicine but it is in my luggage. I need the doc to up my doses. I need to get in counseling too. But I am afraid that I will not be able to share my full worries without the person worrying themselves. I feel like going home and taking down all my awards and uniforms and putting them away. I don't even want to wear my Iraq shirts out of the house because I don't want people asking me about it. They could never understand.

▲▲▲

Mid-October 2006
After speaking with Rebekah last night, I discovered that I was manic while driving and I really didn't care if I died or not. I even ran 8 miles that morning and that wasn't enough. I am feeling down this morning, but I did half the Klonopin. I still want to die but I can't get past the dishonor it would bring to my service and family. I feel that I do not have a purpose that is worth living for. I am constantly consumed with thoughts of killing myself. I cannot handle myself and I am losing control. The only way out is going back to Iraq and being killed.

I guess my medicine is not mood proof. I have little motivation for anything other than golf and eBay. I run because I have to and sometimes it does feel good. I have been back from Iraq for almost 9 months and I am still doing horribly. I feel like killing someone—not excluding myself. I am tired of living if that is really what I am doing. What in the Hell am I doing? I feel that my mind is warped and I am not thinking as a rational person would.

Why am I like this? I miss my buddies yet I cannot be with them.

   I hate this. I am hurting so bad and my mind is flipping out and I don't know how much longer I can hold on. I feel like I'm losing control.

Around the end of October, I started skipping work. Some days I just couldn't get out of bed. It was like having the flu—my body ached from the depression flowing through me like a contagion. Other days I'd go to Starbucks and journal. I took long, very fast drives. I ran, and ran, and ran. Bekah was tired of my endless jogs and the fact that I had stopped helping with the boys. Sometimes I tried, like the weekend afternoon I had Blaine and we met up with my friend Geoff Bailey and his pregnant wife, Sara, for lunch. But the restaurant was so noisy I could barely think, and Geoff and Sara spent so much time interacting with Blaine that the waitress thought he was their son and put his food on their bill.

The one thing I did do with the boys was visit Arlington National Cemetery to pay my respects and show Tyler and Blaine how others had given up their lives for their country. We walked into the Operation Iraqi Freedom area of the cemetery, the boys chattering away with each other. I wasn't sure what I would find but within moments I stumbled onto the tombstone of Brady Westin. I had no idea he had been buried there, and when I saw his name I felt as if someone punched me in the stomach. I put my hands on my knees. My heart was racing and I was sweating. I went silent for several minutes.

"Daddy, what's wrong?" Tyler looked up at me. "Why are you looking at this one?" asked Tyler.

"This was one of my soldiers, Tyler."

There were fresh flowers on the grave.

"I wish I could have helped him more."

"How did he die?" asked Tyler.

I told him he was shot while he was trying to protect people that he had never seen, including his own child.

"That's really bad," said Tyler.

"He wasn't selfish for leaving his family. He died helping other people, including you and Blaine."

Tyler asked me another question but I missed it; half of my mind was far away in Iraq.

Soon their attention was elsewhere. They started to hunt squirrels and as we walked on, I wondered to myself, "What had we done in Iraq that was worth Brady dying for, worth him never seeing the face of his first and only child?"

That night my journal entry was a short transcription from Ecclesiastes (2:17): "*So I hated life, because the work that is done under the sun was grievous to me. All of it is meaningless, a chasing after the wind.*"

Had what we'd done in Iraq been worth anything? Every time I watched the news, the situation was getting worse. I called Geoff one night from my office at Walter Reed. I was still at work, even though I was accomplishing little, and he was already pulling up into his driveway at home after a long commute from our chaplain training. He stayed in his driveway for almost an hour so his wife wouldn't overhear our talk. He was frank with me. He told me I needed help and that he would not hang up until I promised to talk to the VA facility in Coatesville that specializes in PTSD, the one where I had once trained between deployments. He suggested I spend some time there, this time as a patient.

Early November 2006

I am very angry. Toward myself? Toward my group and my supervisor? Toward my wife? Toward my SABRE Family who is not really my family?

I took the day off yesterday because I just could not get myself to go to the hospital. I am having trouble making it through a week of work now.

I am not here today and I want to just curl up and go to sleep.

14

▲▲▲

T R I G G E R   P O I N T S

Early December 2006
I can't believe that I am the patient and not the caregiver.

SOMEONE HAD CARVED *Welcome Home* on a tree stump outside the PTSD building on the Coatesville Medical Facility campus. The first time I saw it I stopped in my tracks. The words were oddly comforting. Even though I was sick, I was being welcomed and was not alone. But I feared its other meaning—that this mental facility *was* my new home, that I belonged here.

When I was admitted to the PTSD unit, a nurse took my vital signs and conducted a Breathalyzer test, all the while jotting notes. After submitting the required urine sample upon check-in, I was escorted to a sterile room with two sinks, two beds, and other military-issue furniture. It was standard procedure to search luggage for contraband, so another nurse tech had me empty most of my luggage onto the small bed. Once I unloaded each of my three bags, she gave me the okay to settle in.

Next to my bed was a simple end table and lamp. I pulled a picture of Bekah and the boys from the pile I had just formed on the bed and propped it up on the table. I missed them terribly and couldn't shake the sense, perhaps the reality, that I was letting them down. I had come to Coatesville to be healed, yet being here already made me feel worthless. Maybe this wasn't a good idea. If neither my family nor my faith could provide any relief from my toxic mind, I wondered if anything could console me.

The other side of the room was messy; there were stacks of paper piled high on the table and the sink hadn't been washed in what looked like weeks. Later I would meet my roommate, Keith: Vietnam vet, peacenik, and political junkie. He was in his fifties, with graying hair. This was his first time at Coatesville but his third decade with PTSD. When I first met him he repeated the message scrawled on the tree stump: "Welcome home."

The window by my bed overlooked the entire medical campus, which hadn't changed at all since my first visit here two years earlier to get training in PTSD counseling. Now, as a patient staring out across the red brick campus, Coatesville felt eerily detached from the real world. It was a forgotten place and its patients—these vets, me—were forgotten, too.

My first hours reminded me of when I convoyed into Tal Afar; I was journeying into the unknown. But this time the unknown was my own mind. There was no adrenaline rush, no joking with other soldiers to relieve our common fears and none of the comfort that comes with being part of a cause outside of yourself. This time I was fighting for my own soul, not for others.

I didn't have much time to think before a nurse came to collect me for an evaluation. She drew my blood and then led me to a smaller office for my primary PTSD screening with about five nurses and doctors who took turns questioning me.

"In the past two weeks have you had thoughts that you'd be better off dead?"

"Yes."

Had I had traumatic experiences in the past that caused me to have intrusive thoughts and nightmares, avoid situations that reminded me of them, be constantly on guard or easily startled, and feel numbed or detached from others?

Yes.

Did I suffer from headaches?

Yes.

I was feeling numb. I responded to the questions in a monotone voice. I don't know what was wrong with me. I had come there seeking help yet at that moment I just wanted to escape the grilling inquiry. Too many staffers were asking me too many questions all at once.

The nurse scribbled notes as the doctors continued with the interview.

My branch of service and role?

Third Armored Cavalry Chaplain. I performed debriefings after deaths, memorial ceremonies, circuit preaching, and counseling in combat.

Noncombat trauma?

Wedgwood Baptist Church in 1999: One night

during evening prayer at a church I attended in Fort Worth, seven people were shot and killed. Bekah and I had switched the nights we regularly attended, so we did not witness the shooting, but certainly did feel its aftermath, from the bare concrete floors where the blood-stained carpets had been pulled up to the prayer services for the killed.

Religion?

I was born Jewish. My mother and stepfather converted and became Baptists and I was raised in the Baptist church.

My verdict?

According to them I lacked the ability to connect with other people in a relationship and had anger and irritability and anger-control issues since returning home from my second tour in Iraq. There were other red flags: loss of motivation, insomnia, frequent intrusive memories, and hypervigilance to the point of being reluctant to drive because of constant road rage.

Did I have nightmares and were they war related?

Yes.

How often?

About four times a month.

My diagnosis?

Ineffective individual coping related to PTSD, determined by isolation, depression, and anxiety.

I was even screened for spiritual issues.

Yes, I answered, spirituality was important to me. I told the nurse I was a pastor, but I didn't tell her I was spiritually void. I was angry at everyone, especially those

I once held dear to me, God included. I didn't want anything to do with anyone, especially myself.

The questions kept coming.

No, I did not have any beliefs that would interfere in my participation in 12-step groups where the term "Higher Power" is used.

Did I want to meet with a chaplain to discuss spiritual or religious issues?

Absolutely not.

▲▲▲

THE VIETNAM VETS I met those first days accepted me warmly and with open arms. But they had been suffering for decades and I was afraid of them and afraid to join their ranks. For some of these vets, it had been forty years since their trauma, which seemed frozen in place, like a photograph that wouldn't fade no matter how hard they tried to rub away its image.

I felt guilty for being at Coatesville. I hadn't been physically wounded; I was here because my mind was weak. Why couldn't I shake my symptoms? Never in my life had I been wholly incapable of fixing a life problem; my solutions in the past might have been slapdash or lacking, but solutions were found. Now, for the first time, failure—both professional and personal—was a very real possibility.

I didn't feel like a chaplain anymore. I felt like a fraud and wanted to run 100 miles per hour in the opposite direction of everything my life had become. I hated what was happening to me and I hated what I had seen in Iraq. What I really hated were clichés, the kind I might hear from staffers, other vets, and from other chaplains or ministers. I hated them because I knew that most of those statements were meant to ease the worries of the speaker, not the one hurting. I had come to discover that clichés were another form of hiding, yet at times even I had fallen prey to their easy charms. Ten years of training as a pastor, six years of active duty as a chaplain—it all began to feel like a giant mistake.

I knew I'd have a hard time making friends at Coatesville. There were about two dozen vets in my ward, most were from Vietnam but six or seven of us were from Iraq. I was the only one still on active duty. During meals I'd sit with a few guys from my floor, but I didn't talk much. Since most of the vets had been enlisted and I was an officer, I was something of an outsider. I even looked uptight. I wore khakis and pastel polo shirts, but most of the vets wore jeans and ripped T-shirts. Some had criminal records, had been through multiple divorces, and had used drugs.

I was also the only chaplain, which made people standoffish. When soldiers are around chaplains, they tend to watch their language, as if we're authority or father figures. I wanted them to treat me like anyone else, but as a chaplain they accorded me extra respect, which I didn't deserve or want. I didn't talk about spiritual matters because I was ashamed of my state of mind when it came to God. I was too embarrassed to tell anyone who didn't already know that I was a chaplain; I would just describe myself as a captain.

Once, I made the mistake of telling one of the nurse techs, who knew my real job, that I wasn't feeling terribly devout. She did exactly what I had feared—she tried to talk me out of my senseless emotions and so I added her to the growing list of people to avoid.

On my second day I met with a social worker for a private session. She was soft-spoken and kind, and sat perched behind her small desk, piled high with the papers of veterans she was trying to help.

She asked the standard questions. Did I need an advance directive, a form you can fill out at hospitals in the event I was to go on life support for any reason. I didn't. Did I wish to meet a VA rep to file for disability? I didn't know the answer to that one; I was still active duty. She suggested I try it anyway just to get information. So I agreed and we set a date.

She asked if my family needed any help, and I said no, I didn't think so. Then she wanted to talk about Bekah.

"Have you two had any recent experiences that might have been very stressful for her?" she asked.

I sat silently. The social worker let the silence fill the room and then asked again. "Any events you'd like to share?"

I thought about it and remembered our first and only date night after moving to Maryland. We had gone to a restaurant at the Washingtonian Center, an upscale outdoor mall in Gaithersburg with its own artificial lake and hordes of happy shoppers. They sat us by the kitchen with my back to the rest of the room. At that point I wasn't aware of what I'd later learn were called trigger points—things that set me off. Having my back to activity and noise was one of them. It was date night but I remember being short with Bekah, even as we were talking about the kids, and I didn't know how to tell her I was uncomfortable there.

"The main problem was the noise. We were right near the kitchen and I could barely hear Bekah."

"Did that ruin your conversation?" she asked.

"Everything took extra effort, it was hard to think. I jumped every time the cookware banged. But the bad part was later, in the parking lot."

"What happened?"

I sighed. I knew I was about to sound like a complete screw-up.

"We walked to the parking lot and it was packed with cars trying to get spots, circling around. Bekah drove, she drives a lot nowadays; before, I always did the driving. She thinks I drive too fast. Anyway, we couldn't back out because the car that wanted our spot was jammed in right behind us, so I told her to go forward—the spot in front of us had just cleared. She started to and then a car came into the spot ahead of us so quickly we almost had a head-on collision. The driver was mouthing some nonsense through the window at us."

"So what did you do?"

"I jumped out of our van and ran up to the driver and started screaming at him."

He had been angry and mouthing off. As soon as I approached his car, he stopped. I couldn't remember exactly what I had shouted, but I remembered a lot of expletives and hand motions. I was in combat mode, fight or flight, and I was ready to fight. I think I scared him. I could feel the evil burning from my eyes and he must have felt it too.

"I guess I scared him, because he rolled up his window and backed right out."

"You're not telling me about what Bekah felt. What did she say to you after this?"

"We both sat there for a long time without saying anything. I needed to let all the stress drain out of me. I think she was just so embarrassed she didn't know what to say."

"How did that make you feel?"

"Like an out-of-control monster."

Yet at the same time I derived some secret pleasure from my outbursts. There were many times in Iraq when I was flooded with adrenaline, and I had come to love the feeling; the parking-lot fight was no different.

"I felt badly for putting Bekah in that situation but mostly I felt far away from her."

I was also done with this counseling session. I felt so tired my eyes must have been closing. I remembered more from that night but didn't want to talk about it any further. I had been sitting right next to Bekah but I might as well have been in Iraq, the gulf between us was so wide. It was as if I had left my body, and all that was left was pure hatred toward all people, including her.

The social worker finished up her notes and said we'd meet again in three days. I walked back to my room and went for a run. After 10 miles I started to feel better. Perhaps it wasn't counseling and medication that would help me; maybe the only therapy I needed was the freedom to run away.

December 2006
For the first time in my life I have an opportunity to sit back and focus on getting better versus taking care of others. I have taken two steps backward by being here. I feel like a failure.

I've been here for two days and I am getting to know the facility and the people better but I am not sleeping well and I am still scared. I want to "hide out" and escape. I was reading my Bible and I found myself getting violently mad at God. I started reading Job, but my anger was triggered when his friends just couldn't be with him and they had to contribute their two-cents. Then I turned the pages to 1 Chronicles and I read about David angering God and God let David choose the Lord's wrath for counting the fighting men in Israel. God sent the Angel's fury and the 70,000 were killed because of one man. How Senseless! What kind of God have I been devoting my life to? Have I wasted 10 years of my life?

This was the first time since seminary that I had the time to question the foundations of my beliefs.

My Bible had always been my comfort, but lately when I opened it, I was flooded with a wave of anxiety and nauseating doubt. My family, Geoff Bailey, Bekah— they were all saying that my time at Coatesville would be "God's watch" over me. Truth be told, I wasn't sure I wanted to be under God's watch. From what I had seen, he wasn't a very responsible caretaker. What kind of God would allow people to sink to the depths we here in this ward had sunk? Perhaps this was the same God who hardened Pharaoh's heart and caused the demise of thousands. This was the same God who told the Israelites to slay everything in Canaan—women, children, and animals. Did it make any sense to rely on that God?

The way that God runs the universe just didn't make sense. How can someone who actually exists stand by and let children suffer? How can He allow extreme evil to touch the lives of the defenseless? I preached in the shade of tanks over bullet-ridden corpses that God would not leave or forsake any of us. Was that a comfort to the mother when she hears of her son's death? Was it a comfort to the wife who finds out for the very first time that her husband is not coming home, or to the small children who learn that they will never know their father or feel his love? Was God standing by me as I isolated myself from my family, so much so that I was now more removed from them that I had been during deployments?

How does it help to know that God is walking with you if He could care less whether you make it across the street?

Sitting on my bed, surrounded by the white emptiness of the mental health ward, I still believed in God. But I didn't see how I could talk to myself or others about His "comforting presence" anymore. Maybe He wasn't comforting or good after all.

Early December 2006
Where do I start? There is so much. I am scared that I will

not be able to work through all of this. I am afraid of
the baggage I have been carrying—I want to unpack it
but I don't.

The problem wasn't only in my mind, no matter what
all the social workers, therapists, and doctors had to say.
It was also in my heart and my nerves. PTSD is an anxiety disorder and my nerves were shot. Somewhere along
the trajectory of my two deployments, I had internalized
the traumas, the deaths, the chaos, and the lack of safety.
I was supposed to be a pillar of strength and support; instead I was a sponge, absorbing all the grief and making it
my own. Now, whether in a parking lot or lost in my
thoughts, I was overreacting to all perceived injustices
around me instead of digesting the circumstances of the
moment and making a rational response. The good thing
was that I knew enough about all this to have a bird's-eye
view—I had trained in this very facility, after all—I just
needed a little help and I'd be back on track. At least
that's what I told myself every morning, afternoon, and
night.

On my tenth day at Coatesville, I finally attended one
of their morning chapel services. The chaplain leading
the service was an elderly Methodist who greeted each of
us, about fifty veterans in total, as we walked in and took
our seats in the wooden pews. I didn't know this wing of
the facility as well as I knew the PTSD ward, which made
me feel out of my depth.

So did his service. I found it hard to follow what he
was saying, as if my brain was going soft on me. I won-

dered if my mystery cup—that vessel into which I would pour all those nagging questions about faith I couldn't answer—was now so lined with cracks, it might just be best to smash the thing. Being in that chapel I felt as if someone had shined a spotlight on me, and I wasn't much of a sight. I didn't want to face God even though I had devoted more than a decade of my life to Him. I had experienced his love and aid yet I wanted to be a million miles away from Him. All I could think about was that I felt naked, as if God could see to my core, and I felt dirty. I was bitter and ugly and didn't recognize myself most mornings in the mirror. "Is it possible," I wondered, "to be scared of *yourself?*"

▲▲▲

MY SCHEDULE WAS as orchestrated and controlled as it had been for the patients I had so recently counseled at Walter Reed. At 8:00 a.m. all of us on the ward watched some form of PTSD video. At 9:00 a.m. on Mondays, Wednesdays, and Fridays we had our smaller group session with Dr. Meredith Currie, where we'd share what was on our minds or discuss the video we had just seen.

Every time I moved it seemed someone was taking notes about me. We were not allowed to leave campus, and I'd revel in my privacy when I got day passes. I'd drive to nearby towns to watch a movie, go to Starbucks or shop for supplies like laundry detergent, noodles, and oatmeal, which I'd eat by myself in our little kitchenette on the ward. At 1:00 we'd have art activities and once a week we'd have recreational therapy, where we'd learn to relieve stress through various hobbies and sports. Twice a week a social worker would lead group sessions on anger management, the type of material I so recently taught as a chaplain.

On Tuesdays and Thursdays I'd have individual sessions with Dr. Currie, who was doing her best to use eye-movement PTSD therapy on me. I would sit upright in a chair as she slowly moved a pencil back and forth horizontally in front of my eyes, with the aim of reconnecting the parts of my brain that are often stunted when trauma occurs. By mimicking the eye movements of sleep during a wakened state, the hope was that my body would launch a healing response it was incapable of doing at night.

"What is your goal?" she asked me, as the pencil waved in front of my eyes.

"My goal . . . is to stop feeling defenseless," I answered.

"What do you picture when you see the event?"

I told her the story of being on the roof—the blinding light, the sudden sound of guns, the realization that I did not have a weapon or any means to fight back, the realization that I was out of my depth and far from home and safety. I told her that a week after that event, an Iraqi translator was shot in the arm on that same roof.

"What negative feelings do you have when you picture yourself on that roof?" she asked.

"I . . . was out of control, I wasn't in control. It's a strange feeling—someone I don't even know is trying to kill me. Someone who has never met me has my life in their hands."

"What would you like to believe about yourself?" she asked.

"That I could fight back. That I could have control over my actions or my safety somehow."

She asked me, on a scale of one to seven, how much control did I believe I had on that roof. I answered, "Three." We did the EMDR, Eye Movement Desensitization and Reprocessing, several more times, and each time my answer was three. Each time we went through the round of questioning, a warm sensation would pass over me, not entirely pleasant, and my heart would pound violently.

"Where do you feel the warm sensation?" she asked.

"In my stomach."

She started another round of the pencil-and-eye movements and then asked if the warm feeling was still there.

"Yes."

Just two years prior I was trained by these same doctors in EMDR yet with all of my training and knowledge, I was unable to progress in therapy. In some ways it was that training that hindered me. I knew the technique too well, I knew something of what was in Dr. Currie's mind as she observed and questioned me. How could I be a patient when I knew all the tricks of the caregiver?

For the first few weeks I didn't know with whom I felt closer, the doctors or the patients. I had been happy to see Dr. Currie at first in the hallways and gave her a big hug as if she were a colleague—which prompted some questions from the other vets—but as the weeks wore on, I wanted to avoid her too.

Even with the therapy my PTSD severity level was rated seven out of ten, still extremely high especially after weeks of treatment. I was making some headway; I started to understand that my trigger points centered around feeling unheard. At the same time I found it hard to voice my anxieties. My anxiety level was also rated high, eight out of ten. But I was getting more comfortable in my new home and was starting to feel safe in the ward. Many days I wished I could stay there forever and dreaded the day when I'd have to check out.

Even though my therapy wasn't progressing well, I could go for days at a stretch without feeling anxious. It's actually not that hard when you finally give up. After months and maybe years of fighting, I was finally caving. I knew that Coatesville was a last-ditch effort for me to heal, but in some ways I just didn't care anymore. I felt myself giving up on my work and my marriage as clearly as if I was letting sand out of my hands and calmly watching it sift away.

I had one bright spot each day, at 1:00 p.m. for one hour. All of the counseling, group sessions, videos, and offers of help from other chaplains had done nothing for me. The only thing that lowered my blood pressure was ceramics.

The ceramics room was filled with multiple shelves of unfinished clay animals, lighthouses, vases, jewelry boxes, and—because it was December—Santas. There were three large tables set up where we could use beads or stencil belts to reshape or decorate the clay into whatever we wanted. We would carefully clean the unfinished ceramics with tiny knives or sandpaper and then paint whatever we had shaped. At the end of each session, we would put our work on a set of shelves where pieces of masking tape with our names reserved space for our art. Then the "art therapists," as they were called, would bake our little projects in the kiln, after which we'd glaze and they'd refire them.

The only sound in that room was the scraping of clay and soft, classical music; it was there that I found the perfect outlet for my hypervigilance. No spot of clay missed my careful knife, no paint ever smudged. From the premade molds I created exactly what my sons needed; I formed Batman out of a cat for Blaine and a Superman out of a frog for Tyler. I made Bekah a collection of bowls with lids and some jewelry boxes. Sometimes I'd take the pottery and some paints back to my room to work on them there, since one hour wasn't always enough.

For me, ceramics were an outlet. For Bekah, I would later learn, my forays into the world of art were profoundly disturbing.

Rebekah Benimoff, January 2006
Another separation. At first it seemed no different from any of the other times he was gone. Except that this time it was a relief since I am no longer under constant fear of attack. I am realizing that until today I did not connect with the reality that Roger is in treatment at the facility in Coatesville. When he began to bring home ceramics on his weekend visits it hit me that he was in a mental facility. On TV you

always see people who are going through various types of
rehabilitation painting or doing art of some sort, and when
I pictured my husband doing this, I began to see the extent of
his brokenness. I feel shocked and have much grief over my
husband being in a psych ward. I never imagined we would
end up in a place like this, and I wonder if he will ever get
better. I wonder why God has allowed this. I love the kids,
but I am tired of being left alone with them all the time. I
know he is not off having fun and I know that he is hurting
and really not in a place where he could care for anyone or
anything, but I need a break and I need some support. It
seems that we're in a place of isolation. I miss my family
and I miss my friends from Ft. Carson. My husband is
falling apart and I have no support here. Father God, I
want to give up, but I won't. Help me dig into you and let
you fill the voids. There are so many.

▲▲▲

WHEN I FIRST came to Coatesville, the days never
seemed to end. Now it felt like weeks were passing without notice.

Once, we took a field trip to the Reading Memorial,
where a group of vets and I read letters to the fallen; mine
was to Private Byrd, who had died of pneumonia. I wrote
that I was thinking of him and that he had fought for a
good cause. But as the days passed and the TV screen in
our group room gave us news of more casualties in Iraq,
I found it hard to remember why we were there in the
first place. Everything we had done in Al Anbar during
my first deployment and then in Tal Afar had seemed so

important at the time, but could we really point to any real success?

I had felt perfect when I was in the battle zone. Every part of my mind and body was in supreme working condition—and I believed so profoundly in the cause, in the chaplaincy, in God, and in myself. As soon as I was back home and the adrenaline wore off, it all unraveled.

We had gone to Iraq because there were weapons of mass destruction stockpiled across the country. Yet those weapons were never found and may never have existed. I had gone to Iraq thinking that was the cause. But if the cause had been wrong, what did that say about our role there, and mine? These questions had eaten away at me for months. After two months with a therapist at Coatesville, however, I was able to reconcile myself to the idea we had done our best in an impossible situation. Soldiers did what has always been their job—to serve their country and be prepared to die for it. I had done my job—to serve the soldiers. If I tried to think too far beyond that simple logic, I might go mad.

I felt I needed more time at Coatesville. I had reconciled my purpose for being in Iraq, but beyond that I was lost. I was angry with God, angry with my wife, and mostly angry and disappointed with myself. "Where do I go from here?" I wondered. I couldn't imagine being anywhere but at this institution. And I certainly couldn't see how I could ever be a chaplain again.

Late January 2007
Another day is almost over. I took my meds and I should be sleeping soon. I don't like people anymore nor do I like

talking about religion. It strikes me as something I have cre-
ated in order to be accepted in life. I needed God in order to
make it through difficult times and for protection. I needed
God for safety. I am alive today and I made it through hard
times. So can I say that God came through for me? Can I
say that I was protected and he was faithful when I was not?
Why am I so angry? I do not want anything to do with God.
I am sick of religion. It is a crutch for the weak. You have to
be weak-minded to follow such a thing. My interpretation,
your interpretation, we make God into what we need for the
moment. I hate God. I hate all those who try to explain God
when they don't really know.

15

▲▲▲

HOMECOMING

Late January, 2007

*My PTSD symptoms have decreased by 20% and I will be
discharged soon. I made a little progress. I am starting to
come to grips with a different me that has to operate differently than I did before the deployments. But I am still scared
about going back to work and going home. I still blow up at
a moment's notice. I have been back from Iraq 3 days and 1
year. My anxiety is high and my stomach is burning.*

PART OF ME wanted to stay indefinitely in my cave called
Coatesville. But when it was time to check out for good, I
managed to take some of Coatesville with me. Workers
had been replacing the slate roofs of several older buildings and I had my eye on some of their material. One
chilly February morning I walked outside to one of their
Dumpsters and, praying they wouldn't notice, climbed
inside and sifted through hundreds of pieces of broken
slate to find two that would fit my requirements—they

had to be about at least a foot and a half long and one foot high. None of the workers, who were nearby eating lunch, said a thing. Perhaps they thought all of us at Coatesville were unhinged. They were probably more afraid of me than I was of them.

I carried the slate back to our ceramics room, with a plan.

Dr. Currie had been working with me to "reframe" the meaning of my time in Iraq, to accept my limitations and those of everyone around me. Part of doing that meant having something that would remind me every day of what had been gained and lost during my deployments. For the past few months, that daily reminder had come in the form of a nightmare or anxiety attack and I needed something new, fast. I also knew that if I was going to "reframe" my time in Iraq, I would have to do so with my hands, with a memorial. I wondered how many vets had received care under the auspices of the slate as I slid it under the faucet of a large sink. I scrubbed the dirt off with a yellow sponge and dried the pieces with rough, brown paper towels. For me these were holy pieces of slate and they needed to be perfectly cleansed.

I decided to paint a second squadron "Cavalry Guidon" on the first slate. A guidon is a banner carried by cavalry regiments into battle. Guidons date back to Biblical times and are extremely symbolic for the Army. In centuries past they were blessed before missions, where they served as rallying points for fighting units. Even if all the soldiers should die, the guidon was supposed to survive any attack and be transferred through the generations.

I had painted and etched so many ceramics that by now I was something of a pro in the little world of Coatesville. I gathered paints and 2-inch stencils and spent the next two hours laying tape to create straight lines and markers for the guideon. I painted the upper half a deep red, several coats, and let it dry overnight. The next morning I perfected the white lower half. Centered on the red portion I stenciled a number 3 to represent the Third Armored Cavalry. Centered on the white portion I stenciled a number 2 for second squadron, my squadron. On the right-hand portion of the slate, I personalized it by painting, in cursive *In Memoriam, To Those Who Sacrificed All*.

I had a simpler design for the other placard, which would read *The Benimoffs*.

Most of the time I wished I could cut myself off from everything—including Bekah—but I knew my mental state wasn't stable. When I had been home for Valentine's Day I yelled at her, though now I couldn't remember why. I couldn't remember the last time we made love; it would have been before we moved to Maryland eight months earlier. At my darkest moments I wondered if the deployments had helped our marriage only because it gave us time away from each other. Now we'd be back in the same house with no looming deployments. I often thought about divorce, about getting a small apartment for myself and disappearing into it, leaving only to buy food and other essentials. She and I had changed so much, I didn't see where our hearts could meet again. But I told myself that now that I had learned about my trigger points, if I could just minimize my reactions to them, I might be able to go back to being my old self. I knew I was being unfair to her. I also realized that if I failed both as a chaplain and as a husband at the same time, I might not survive the collapse. So I vowed to turn myself around and do better.

I wanted the slate to represent unlimited possibilities for my family, so I etched the Statue of Liberty to the left of where I would write *The Benimoffs*. I methodically painted the deep blue ocean surrounding Manhattan. My father lives in Staten Island, and my sister and I spent two summers with him when we were kids. I always remembered the ferry rides he took us on; they were like magic ocean voyages. The statue was a symbol of hope for millions of immigrants, but for me it had symbolized my dream that my father would want to be my dad again, that somehow we'd find a way to become a real family. That never happened. But now I had a family of my own and we needed to start a new life together. Feeling sorry for missing most of the Christmas holidays, I painted a green wreath in the upper right corner. Painting *The Benimoffs* by hand proved to be a difficult feat. I had to paint freehand since we didn't have any cursive stencils and it took three times to get it right. As I painted I told myself I was going to work to make things right at home as well.

I left Coatesville on a cold Wednesday morning in late February. During my final weeks I had gotten to know many of the other patients, mostly Vietnam vets, and I would once again miss the camaraderie—this time of being around people with the same, shared disability. I felt much like I had when I returned home from my second deployment—alone and re-entering a world infinitely more unpredictable than where I was coming from.

In the backseat of the Toyota, I carefully laid the two placards. That first hour of the ride I felt calm and in control. By the second hour I was plagued with doubt. What were Bekah and the boys expecting from me? I was damaged goods and had no idea what role I was supposed to fill. In my past life I had been a father, a husband, a chaplain, and a believer. Now I didn't fit any of those roles; they felt like made-up characters. I didn't know where I was headed; I just knew that the exits and off-ramps were taking me to a place that was supposedly my home.

When I pulled up the driveway, the boys came running out with Bekah close behind. We all hugged and I tried to act cheery. The boys and I tumbled on the grass and when I unloaded the car, I proudly showed them the placards. They pretended to be impressed, but I could see through their effort. We were all putting on a show. I told myself I shouldn't expect them to appreciate the memorials as much as I did, that kids, not dads, bring home art, but their reaction stung nonetheless.

We settled down to chat in the living room where Bekah asked politely about the drive. The boys, I suspected, had been coached to ask how I was feeling. Then they described to me in detail all the new games they had conjured up in my absence. Within twenty minutes I explained I ought to go upstairs and unpack to feel settled, but the truth was that I already needed a break. I sat on the edge of the bed and heard them talking downstairs; the boys wanted to escape to their playroom and Bekah let them free.

I remembered how before coming home from Tal Afar, Bekah and I had talked about our expectations of each other. It had been my idea. But this time there had been no such talk. She had given up on negotiating with me. Her only agreement—that she wouldn't consider leaving me now—was between her and God. I, meanwhile, had no such arrangements with God or anyone else. I was not talking to God because I had nothing good to say. I still believed in God, but not necessarily a compassionate one and perhaps not one to whom I should be devoting my life.

I tried to buy some time by shutting myself in the bathroom for a few minutes. I just couldn't get over the fact that my life had changed so dramatically, so quickly. Instead of seeing a thirty-four-year-old chaplain and family man when I looked in the mirror, I saw an aged, failed person.

When I finally went downstairs again, Bekah seemed anxious too. She offered to make sandwiches while I hung the placards. Hiding in the garage I found my tools and drilled two small holes into each, hanging the Benimoff sign by our front door and the cavalry placard over the garage entrance. Each time I parked I planned to study that memorial before going inside. That way, I figured, I could honor our service but wouldn't bear the weight of Iraq on my shoulders every time I walked in my front door.

That first night home I woke up from a nightmare

with a fuzzy memory of having been in Iraq and under fire, fear still coursing through my body. On the second day, surrounded by manicured lawns and giggling children, I had guilty thoughts about the soldiers killed during my two deployments. I felt a vague sense of my betraying all of them by living past them, by never taking the risks they had, by being a chaplain and not a soldier when what they needed was armed backup, not gentle words.

And what *were* all those words I had so easily let roll from lips while in Iraq? How could God have been watching over us? I returned and they didn't return. How can I say God protected me when the other guys didn't come back? Did God not protect them? What kind of man would I be if I said to myself God had been watching over me but not over them?

That was one of the reasons I couldn't go to church; I couldn't stand to hear that phrase any longer—"God was watching over me." He wasn't watching over the good men I knew in Iraq. Faith was the center of my life yet it failed to explain why I came home and those soldiers did not. The phrase was a Christian nicety, a cliché that when put to the test didn't fit reality.

▲▲▲

WITHIN FOUR DAYS I'd be back at Walter Reed, so I tried to stay calm by focusing on simple chores. I straightened the garage, hung pictures, and vacuumed. Bekah and I circled each other carefully, ever polite. I didn't want to argue and she didn't either. We were much like a sputtering motor that couldn't decide if it wanted to stall or go. I had spent so much time alone that it was odd to be surrounded by family. And I was unnerved to be living so close to a person I was supposed to be passionate about, when I couldn't muster any of those feelings. With the boys it was easier, but in small doses. When they came home from school, I would wrestle with them, making a point of rubbing my new scratchy goatee on their cheeks. It drove them into wild howls, but just as we'd start to have fun, I'd need a break. I kept ruminating on the same question: How could I be with those whom I loved when I was so hateful?

Coatesville had done several things for me: I learned about my condition, discovered what my trigger points were, and redefined my purpose in Iraq. But none of that made me less angry. I had told my therapist I had reached the point where I despised the notion of helping people. I told her that being around wounded soldiers just flooded me with negative emotions: fear, sadness, grief, rage over the injustice of it all. It was better for everyone if I just kept to myself.

But what I did with myself was waste precious time and resources. Before Coatesville, one way I hid was on the computer. It was the only way I could technically be at home but escape at the same time. I had avidly bought and traded golf equipment on eBay (despite knowing that a common PTSD trait is to spend large sums of money) and went to the driving range instead of being a parent or a husband. For sixty dollars I had played golf twice a week, which didn't seem too bad. But when I couldn't fit that in our budget, I charged it. I hid the credit card bills

HOMECOMING 203

from Bekah, but while I was at Coatesville she finally caught on. In just a few months I had racked up ten thousand in debt. I promised her there would be no more wild spending, but on my third day home I was back on eBay; it was an addiction.

On Sunday morning she took the boys to their new church, a chapel in Silver Spring which I had never been to. She kept glancing at me as they got dressed and walked out the door, hoping at the last minute I'd jump in the car with them. She knew it was pointless to invite me outright. I didn't want to be packed in a large, crowded auditorium and I didn't trust a stranger to preach to me about how God was by my side. I felt her disappointment from outside as the door quietly shut behind her.

That night Bekah and I did work out a new arrangement we thought might help when I started work again. From now on, when I came home I'd have thirty minutes alone to destress. It was one thing for our marriage to have problems, it was another thing altogether when I couldn't handle time with the boys. I realized I often thought of them as stimuli, not as my children. Half the time I was scared of them. That's because they were typical little boys; they were always eager to run around and scream, like little IEDs firing off without any notice.

One week into our new routine, I knew I was falling desperately below any and all expectations. My whole goal in seeking help—the counseling, the medications, my time at Coatesville—was to be able to return to my family as a father and as a husband. Bekah had the same expectation, and for that had accepted my "third" deployment, to Coatesville. Perhaps we had both had the same high hopes that I'd come home happy and smiling, and with those dashed hopes came anger. I wasn't the man she had married and she was losing patience.

I could sense disappointment filling the house and the only thing I could think to do was to walk upstairs and shut the door.

▲▲▲

I HAD CHANGED, but so had Walter Reed. Only nine days before my return as a chaplain, the *Washington Post* ran the first of a series of articles about mismanagement at Walter Reed, and a full-blown scandal was brewing. The stories told of veterans of Iraq and Afghanistan living among mice, mold, rot, and cockroaches at Building 18 (an off-campus site I had never visited). But worse, according to the reports, were the allegations of negligence. Wounded soldiers had to fight for disability payments or meetings with doctors. Some of them were being forgotten altogether at different sites on the 113-acre campus.

I was walking into an institutional crisis. I'll speak for myself when I say it felt like everything was broken. If the system was broken, so was I—a broken healer for broken soldiers in a broken system. God save us all.

With congressional hearings looming and an embarrassed President Bush insisting that Walter Reed fix whatever was wrong ASAP, our commander was fired on March 1. Over the next few weeks, the signature ink would still be wet on documents as supervisors came and went.

When I first walked into my office, Geoff Bailey was there to greet me, as were several Christmas gifts covered with dust: an ornament, some books on spending time with kids, and a my favorite—a T-shirt that read "I didn't lose my mind, I sold it on eBay." I was touched that people had thought about me while I was gone, but I also felt embarrassed about the reason for my absence.

The mood at Walter Reed was grim. Many officers and NCOs were getting fired and those who remained did not know how secure their jobs were. The head chaplain of Walter Reed briefed us that we needed to be extrasensitive to veterans but also to the doctors, nurses, and other employees; to make sure that we'd be present if they also needed to talk, given the extra pressure. He stressed that we live up to our requirements—which included seeing a patient within seventy-two hours of their arrival. Everyone at Walter Reed would be under scrutiny and it would be important to carry out our jobs better than ever. These were all good orders, except that I knew I was not up to the task.

On March 8 the Army's vice chief of staff announced a reorganization of a program at Walter Reed designed to guarantee that wounded soldiers would no longer fall through the cracks. The program was called the "Wounded Warrior Transition Brigade" and would now expand to bring in combat-seasoned officers and noncommissioned officers to help streamline care for Walter Reed's nearly seven hundred outpatients. Instead of all seven hundred being in one unit, they would be divided into three units, each with its own chaplain on call 24/7, overseen by a brigade chaplain.

Since I'd been away I was one of the few chaplains in my training group not already assigned to a specific position on campus. For that reason I was immediately assigned to one of the new units, approximately two hundred patients, most of them at Mologne House and three other hotels centrally located on campus. In addition to counseling, I was to help ensure that the wounded warriors had decent housing on campus and were able to focus on healing, not just bureaucratic entanglements over care and compensation. I thought it might be better for everyone if I didn't focus my pastoral care on Iraq soldiers, especially without the comfort of my group, but I seemed to have little choice. One would think that you'd want a functional chaplain to minister to those who are dysfunctional. Perhaps they hoped my problems would make me a better minister, or that by rising to the challenge I would snap out of my own dysfunction. But I had spent the past three months isolated and protected from the real world, and now I was being thrust back into it, with the nation's media, Congress, and everyone else watching every move at Walter Reed. I hadn't resolved questions about my faith or Iraq, so how could I help others tackle those same issues?

The second article in the *Washington Post* series, which went on to win a Pulitzer Prize for investigative reporting, was about the Mologne House. It was an old hotel, with chandeliers, a bar, and a cozy lobby. But instead of the usual hotel crowd, the lobby was filled with young men in wheelchairs, either missing limbs, covered with bandages, or lost in a fog of anti-anxiety medications, the only escape from the reality of their horribly interrupted lives.

The guests of this surreal hotel, as the *Post* wrote, had ears melted off and faces tattooed by shrapnel. "Malogne House is afloat on a river of painkillers and antipsychotic drugs . . . pill bottles clutter the nightstands: pills for depression and insomnia, to stop nightmares and pain, to calm the nerves . . . Here at Hotel Aftermath, a crash of dishes in the cafeteria can induce seizures in the combat-addled. If a taxi arrives and the driver looks Middle Eastern, soldiers refuse to get in. Even among the gazebos and tranquility of the Walter Reed campus in upper Northwest Washington, manhole covers are side-stepped for fear of bombs and rooftops are scanned for snipers."

Perhaps I should be living here, I thought. Every day I swallowed a pharmacy worth of pills. Wellbutrin for anxiety and Effexor for depression, Trazodone to help me sleep, and Seroquel for nightmares. And every day I walked from my office in the old Red Cross building over to Malogne House to be with my own kind.

Inside Malogne House the rooms were tiny and nerves were frayed. When I walked in, my stomach would tighten at the sight of all those injured soldiers crammed together. Often I'd detour to the mini-PX and pretend to browse for toiletries before being able to strike up conversations with soldiers in the lobby. I quickly learned to stay outside the building as much as I could.

Soon my first stop each day was the reflecting pool just behind Malogne House. It was long and rectangular, surrounded by tall trees and rolling grass. Lily pads and large colorful fish, some white with red spots, others pure gold, floated at its surface. I loved watching the fish and was always so grateful they were there. The sound of the pond's small waterfalls soothed me, as it did the soldiers who lazed on benches near the pond, soaking up the sun and smoking or talking the hours away. In the breezeway I'd often see families—many of the soldiers lived in cramped quarters at the Malogne House with wives or, if they were younger, their mothers—cooking hot dogs and burgers in the barbecue pits, their paper cups and plates set up on metal picnic tables.

One day I sat at one of the tables with a young medic who had been shot from the side; a bullet had traveled through one cheek and made a clear exit out the other one. His jaw had just been reconstructed and was now wired shut. Sitting outside with his parents, he was desperate to talk. He told me through his wiring what had happened to him. He was conducting first aid on a soldier when he felt the sting of the bullet shooting through this face. He was matter of fact; he had done what he had to do and was proud to serve. I wondered if he had dealt with the emotional trauma in a healthy way but I wasn't going to press him, I wasn't up to it. I told him I was proud to serve beside him and was humbled by him. I sensed that—like me—he was happier in the role of caregiver than patient. I prompted his parents, who were sitting with him, to talk about whatever they wanted. They were just thankful they hadn't lost their son. I didn't ask about faith or offer to pray with them. They were a happy, close family surviving a terrible ordeal. I should have been inspired. Instead, I struggled to reflect their upbeat attitude while I felt myself sinking.

A few days later I was chatting with a soldier when my Trauma Team pager suddenly beeped. I looked down at the screen: "Code Blue in post surgery recovery room." The trauma team was comprised of surgeons, doctors, nurses, and whichever chaplain was on call; that day it was me. My job could mean many things during a trauma: to support the medical staff if they needed it, to stand at the edge of the bed if a patient was cognizant, to pray with him if he asked for it, and to counsel any family members present.

I raced to the recovery room where a handful of doctors were trying to revive a soldier. He had just been wheeled out of a routine procedure when he had suddenly gone into cardiac arrest.

I chose to stay out of the way as the doctors were frantic and I didn't want to compromise the soldier's care in any way. After about forty-five minutes, the doctors still circled the bed but were no longer running back and forth. The soldier hadn't made it.

Rarely did a soldier die in the recovery room after a routine surgery, and everyone was in a state of shock. I knew my next, most important step would be working with his family. I discovered they were not at Walter Reed, and, to make matters worse, the hospital commander and I soon learned that his parents—who were out of state—had been notified but told to go to the wrong medical center, not here. I was horrified by the mistake, but I also understood where it came from. Everyone was overwhelmed, not just me. The error was quickly fixed and within a few hours the parents and the soldier's brother were en route to Walter Reed with a chaplain escort. Meanwhile, I flew through the paperwork and calls it took to get the family military orders for a room on campus. I called the Malogne House for vacancies, called the office in charge of cutting family orders, and dashed over to the new Soldier and Family Center at the hospital to see what other resources we could pull together before the family arrived. I was in my version of "combat mode"—moving at light speed to close all the gaps before the shocked family stepped foot on campus. I felt I was being productive and solving problems for others. It was the best I'd felt about myself in a long time.

The phone had been glued to my ear for hours when I was paged to see the supervisory chaplains in charge of Walter Reed. I was the chaplain on duty but this was a sensitive case—a routine surgery and a dead soldier with misplaced parents. I immediately briefed them about the arrangements I had made along with the hospital deputy commander in order to get the family settled.

My supervisor interrupted me, "Are you aware of how much anxiety you're showing right now?"

I felt like I had been punched in the ribs and struggled to stay focused on faces staring at me. I realized sweat was pouring through my uniform and I was so jittery that I couldn't stand still. I had regressed into my hypervigilant mode and hadn't even noticed.

I paused. It wasn't smart to admit feeling overwhelmed, but clearly it was obvious.

Yes, I was feeling anxious.

My supervisors were worried about me escorting the family once they arrived later that evening. They would be in shock and would need someone to manage their grief and probable anger. Could I handle that meeting? Their eyes bore into me.

A wave of hot disappointment rushed through my body. I realized that I wasn't able to be of service to the family as they viewed their son's body and afterward. I would be a hindrance, not a help. My supervisors knew this before I did and my heart sank. They would get another chaplain on board. I would still be on call, but my work on this case had quickly come to a close.

I walked out of the office trying not to dissolve in tears until I was out of their sight and safely in the chaplain on-call room. Never before had my limits as a chaplain, as an empathetic human, struck me so violently and quickly. I had read and studied and preached on moments like these but it didn't make going through the experience any easier. I realized that I could not "suck it up and drive on," and for that I started to weep.

I was bankrupt as a person and as a pastor. Not only had I stopped conversing with God, but I continued to put myself above Him. In my mind I had either stood toe-to-toe with Him and challenged Him or ignored Him completely. There were no answers to the questions I kept posing: Why was this all happening to me and to people like me? Was it the fault of the war planners? The fault of the Iraqis? My fault for being so permeable? God's fault? I had spent the past year trying to make sense out of the senseless and at that moment I finally

realized an answer wasn't coming any time soon. So I
wept and as I did I started to talk. It came out like a mum-
ble, but I said it: "I need you." For the first time in
months I realized I was powerless to change and I needed
someone to accept me as the broken person I had become.

That's when I remembered the notion of grace I
needed God's grace more than I needed answers. It's a
lesson from Sunday school, the most basic of all, but one
I had lost sight of completely since returning from Iraq:
*"For it is by grace you have been saved, through faith—and
this not from yourselves, it is the gift of God—not by works, so
that no one can boast" (Ephesians 2:8–9).*

I had read that passage a million times in my years in
seminary and beyond, but hadn't turned to it in years.
God's grace gives a person space to "just be" and not "fix"
an unfixable situation. The Apostle Paul's words also
came to mind: "In my weakness, He is made strong."
Maybe I no longer had to offer a disclaimer for my inad-
equacies. I could be who God created me to be and that,
right now, was a wounded healer. I had become so self-
absorbed and arrogant in my grief that I had lost sight of
my humanity. Believers can depend on a creator who is
willing to love them and forgive them as they navigate
the unforgiving highs and lows of real life. It took being
completely defeated to realize that I was not equal to
God in my bitterness and anger.

I knew this wouldn't change my anger, but it might
change the way I viewed myself. What I needed was
something that wouldn't come from myself, my work,
Coatesville, or my family. Allowing grace back into my

life, I prayed, would fill the void between perfection and failure that I had been disappearing into for a year.

▲▲▲

THE DEPLOYMENTS HAD changed me. Now, for the first time, I recognized how much they had changed Bekah. She had gotten used to operating as a single mother, and, out of necessity, had developed new habits for our family. One of them was a routine with the boys I had found so rigid I often resented it. Each night involved baths, bedtime snacks, tooth brushing, potty, and then bedtime story, in that precise order. Since nights with the boys were the only time I had with them, I often wanted to bend the rules. Now I let go and followed Bekah's lead. It was a relief and I quickly realized they needed the schedule.

I used a similar tactic within my chaplain training group. One of the chaplains had always upset me with his politics. I used to let that anger infect all of my dealings with him but now I tried to focus on what I respected in him, which was his devotion to family. I didn't have all the answers either, so what right did I have to judge him for his views? I could feel myself becoming more reasonable and human, bit by bit. As I gave grace I felt myself receiving it as well, in little ways that made each day more manageable.

A few weeks later I had a checkup with my psychiatrist, Dr. Lehman.

Dr. Lehman handled my medications, had done the paperwork to get me to Coatesville, and perhaps knew me better than I knew myself. In earlier meetings I had admitted to him that my visits with veterans were taking on a superficial tone and that I was starting to feel more like a social worker than a chaplain. I couldn't find it within me to explore their faith in relation to their experiences, because my own faith was unrecognizable. It would have felt like fraud. Now, he shocked me again, just as he had months earlier when he first diagnosed me with chronic PTSD.

"You might start thinking about a medical board," he suggested. A medical board helps evaluate whether soldiers will be discharged or stay on active duty based on their medical condition. Several other committees must meet, but if the soldier is found unfit, the Army then calculates the soldier's retirement amount, and is let go.

Lehman meant that I should consider getting out of the Army because of my PTSD. Walter Reed was under fierce scrutiny on many points, including how long it took medical boards to out-process soldiers and the low disability percentages they were receiving. At that time, the boards were hypersensitive and were awarding better percentages. It was a good time to leave.

"What would I do if I didn't do this? This is my life."

"I'm concerned you are unable to do your job. If things get worse, then we may need to initiate it."

I sat there in amazement. What he said made perfect sense; my heart wasn't in my ministry. At the same time, I had always been in the military. I had enlisted straight out of high school, and now—fifteen years later—the Army was my life. I felt the same way I had when I saw his

PTSD diagnosis of me on his computer screen. My heart stopped and that same warm sensation moved through my body, as if I was about to be conveniently swept away from everything that had once seemed to comprise the makeup of my life.

"Just think about it and let me know," was all Dr. Lehman said.

I left his office and my head was spinning. Okay, think about logistics, I told myself. What would I do—go to law school? Bekah would have to work full-time, but how could she when just managing Tyler's diabetes was a full-time job? I peered into Chaplain David O'Connor's office, which was filled with books and papers. It was around three in the afternoon and he was checking e-mails.

I knocked on the door.

"Sir, can we talk?"

He looked up at me. "Sure." I walked in and sat on his couch, he stopped typing and moved to a chair by the couch.

"What's going on?"

I told him about the talk with Dr. Lehman, and he seemed suspiciously unsurprised by it.

He watched and waited for me to speak.

"I don't know what to do anymore. Maybe he's right. Half the time I hate people, how can I be good at ministry?"

"Maybe you shouldn't rush," Chaplain O'Connor said.

I shouldn't rush. But let's be honest, I told myself. I

was sinking. Anger flooded back into me. Anger at God and anger at the Army, which pushed people too far and then dropped them once they were broken.

I told him how I had let my ministry consume my personal life.

"But I can't talk to Bekah because it's too tense at home," I told him. "I don't understand any of this. I don't want to serve God anymore and I can't have real conversations with patients because I feel false with them."

Chaplain O'Connor let me ramble, never offering cheap answers or clichés. Much later, as I was going, he left me with one parting question.

"Can you be mad at God and still serve Him?"

▲▲▲

I DROVE HOME, stared up at my Third Armored Cavalry plaque, and walked in through the garage and laundry room to the kitchen. Bekah was washing dishes and gave me a strained smile when I walked in.

"I'm through," I told her.

Bekah had a bowl in her hand she was loading into the dishwasher. She understood immediately that I was leaving the Army or that they were leaving me. I could see stress forming a knot in her forehead.

"I can't do it anymore."

She just watched me.

"Dr. Lehman suggested a medical board. He said if there is any time to go through it, it would be now when everything is being scrutinized. It's up to me to decide." I wanted to tell her how I felt: overwhelmed, confused, unable to provide for my family, but I could not communicate any of that to her.

"How much time would it take to process you out?" she finally asked. She was reeling, trying to figure out in that split second which questions to ask me, which to wait and pose to God—her only soulmate since my illness had set in. I didn't know the answer to her question, but I figured it would be a matter of just a few months.

Bekah stepped over to where I was standing a few feet from the fridge.

"What do you want to do?" she asked me slowly.

Maybe, I suggested, I could try law school. Maybe not be a chaplain anymore. I had always the loved the idea of right and wrong, of justice. But that would mean Bekah having to go back to work as a kindergarten teacher.

She just nodded and gave me the hand signal to "wait" as she walked out to the living room and ushered the boys upstairs to brush their teeth.

When she came back she spoke in a whisper. At this point, I realized that she saw me as her third child. Someone she no longer expected to make sense.

"Roger, I understand. But you have to think. You know how much time I spend up at the school taking care of Tyler. And what you don't know is how much time I spend on the phone with medical-supply companies and doctors. I spend my life tracking blood-glucose levels, making adjustments, changing out the insulin in his pump. Not to mention how much time I spend every week just making sure he eats when he should and checks his blood sugar, and gives himself the right amount of insulin. You are not capable of handling this if I'm off at work."

She was overwhelmed, and rightly so. I had dragged my family into so much and now this. I'm sure she thought me capable of all sorts of emotional violence toward my family, and she was within her rights; I had been that person but I was ready to be better. But instead of explaining to her that I understood, I just felt myself fly away from the moment, far away from the discussion I had started.

"We'll figure something out," I said.

"That means that *you* are going to have to go to his school when there is a problem. You won't even learn how to manage the diabetes."

Since coming home from Iraq, I hadn't been involved in programming his diabetes pump. Bekah would meet alone with his doctor and program the different ratios that distributed the amount and timing of his insulin. I helped Tyler when he needed it, but I was far removed from the intricate details of his condition. Now I was the one who couldn't say anything.

"This isn't just about Tyler. You'd have to step up and take care of both of them. You know what my schedule was like when I taught full time. You will have to get the kids ready for school, pack their lunches. You will have to cook them dinner . . . and *homework* . . . you know how Tyler fights that! Are you ready to tackle that job? I won't be able to if I am getting home at six . . . or even later." What she didn't say out loud was that she no longer trusted me with them.

"Okay, OKAY!! I don't want to talk about the details

right now." I wanted to leave not just the Army but my entire life. I had opened the floodgates of her own anxieties and couldn't handle them, much less my own.

"These are important things to consider," she continued. "This is the reality of what you getting out actually means."

"I said I don't want to talk about this anymore." I left her there and walked upstairs. I wanted to hide. I didn't want full-time care of the kids. I couldn't even handle their frenetic energy for more than fifteen minutes at a time. I shut myself into the small office and stared at the blank computer screen. I was stuck.

I needed grace. Please, from somewhere. Why was it all or nothing? Serve God and be a perfect believer or get out of ministry altogether. Maybe saying I needed God's grace was just an easy way to rationalize lower expectations of myself.

Instead of reaching for my Bible, which I might have done in years past, I pulled a different book off the shelf. It was about marathon running. At that moment I desperately needed to run. Whether I'd be running from God or to God, I couldn't say.

Rebekah Benimoff, Mid-March 2007
It continues to be so challenging to walk by faith. Roger is struggling at work, and emotionally not present at home. I can see he is under a great deal of stress, and there is so much uncertainty as to our future. Will we stay in the Army? Will he retire? Roger is seriously considering getting a medical discharge.

I wonder how long the process would last. We have esti-

mates, but no facts. Asking for facts could jump-start the process before Roger is completely sure he wants to take this route. What would this mean as far as medical coverage for the kids . . . especially Tyler??? We have to have really good insurance to cover all his diabetic supplies. I do not really want Roger to get out. I'm not ready to go back to work . . . but I do not want Roger to be miserable, either. I confess I am afraid of the unknown.

Lord, help me to not fear so much. Help me to stop worrying about timing and finances and medical coverage! Please help me to let go of all material comforts and simply trust you. I've enjoyed the freedom of not working. Of being comfortable on Roger's salary and not making material sacrifices. With all my heart I want to be able to say—"You, Lord, are sufficient."

WALKING WOUNDED

Rebekah Benimoff, notes for leader's discussion at a Bible study group, May 2007
Having faith is about relationship . . . not answers.

It is not about saying, "Everything is going to be OK," or even, "God has a plan . . . This is all just part of his plan."

The truth of the matter is that we do not like suffering and so we tell ourselves these things in order to try to comprehend the Un-comprehendable. Faith is looking at the realities of the situation and saying, this is more than I can bear, and hearing God when he says,

"That is precisely the point!"

Faith is not about the absence of questioning. For me it has been very much about questioning. And accepting my husband as he works through his own questions.

He does not want us to come to Him once we have everything finally resolved. He wants us to choose relationship despite the unanswered questions.

BEKAH DID NOT want me to quit. It would mean she'd have to go back to work, and that I—in my state—would pick up the extra care for our boys. That wasn't the only reason she wasn't ready for the change. She feared that my leaving the chaplaincy might lead me to abandon my faith altogether. At that point, she would have to admit that I was no longer the man she married.

I tried to stay afloat at Walter Reed while I delayed making a decision about staying in the chaplaincy. Throughout all my years in the Army, helping soldiers had been my driving force. Now I wanted to run from them. When I saw injured soldiers, I felt physically defeated; my stomach turned and my vision blackened with rage at this system that seemed to chew them all up. I did my best in my counselings, but I felt unable to make a difference in the face of all this tragedy around me. In years past I had thought my pastoring could really help people; now I just tried to make each day slightly less of a failure than the day before.

I no longer avoided these problems by skipping work like I had before Coatesville, and at the end of each day I tried to remember something positive that had taken place. I might not be feeling well, I told myself, but if I could help a soldier with an administrative or emotional problem, at the very least I would be fulfilling some basic function. It was the soldiers, not me, who were strong, optimistic, and capable.

Faced with the prospect of everything I'd worked for slipping away, I clung to the routines that had once filled my life, just to gain some time. How much time, though,

would it take before I knew what step to take next? I felt
like I needed an eternity. I flipped between anger, exhila-
ration, and depression every few hours, and the chemical
ups and downs didn't help my resolve or clear my thinking. By night I was so drained that I couldn't sleep, leading to yet another day of pretending to live my life,
hoping those around me would remember my past deeds,
not my present failures.

When your life feels like a sham, there is little emotional difference between work and home. Your failings
stare you in the face at every turn, even where you are
supposed to feel most comfortable. For me, home was actually worse. If I lashed out, it would be at the people I
was supposed to feel love for. Would I ever be able to
enjoy my family again, and they me?

We settled into something of a half-life. Bekah was
starting to ask questions again, after months of avoiding
conversation or eye contact with me. Before, when she
asked simple questions, like "I'm going to the store, do
you want some milk?" or "Tyler has a parent conference
today, do you want to come?" I would launch into a
heated rant that within seconds would turn to the subject
of Iraq and how much pressure I was under, nothing that
had to do with Tyler or with milk. Now I could answer
them, but the answer more often than not was still that I
wanted to be alone.

Bekah had read all the material I brought home from
Coatesville, and she tried to help the boys understand, in
their own way, that their father was going through a traumatic time. She read them a children's version of a PTSD

brochure called "Why Is Daddy Like He Is?" "Daddy
has lost a lot of friends," she told them. "If you lost a lot
of your friends, how would you feel?" She asked them
what they were noticing about me. "He's mad all the
time and doesn't want to be with us," said Tyler. "Daddy
yells a lot," added Blaine. When Blaine went to sleep,
Bekah read Tyler more of the medical literature on
PTSD, explaining more of the symptoms. One night
Tyler asked her, "Is that why Daddy doesn't care about
us anymore?"

It had been hard for Bekah to separate my diagnosis
and need for self-care from a convenient excuse to do
whatever I wanted, like go on long runs or sit at the computer for hours at a time. In Iraq the idea of self-care had
struck me as egocentric. I'd take some minimal time to
myself, to work out or read, but it had made me feel
guilty to relax when I knew my soldiers couldn't. At home
I had reversed course. All I could focus on was myself,
and my own sons detected my selfish behavior. Even
though for the first time in months I was trying to spend
more one-on-one time with them, I was still far from the
father I had once been.

I was still embarrassed about my PTSD symptoms
and asked Bekah not to tell anyone at her church about
my disorder. She only confided in a few friends and
prayer partners, many of whom were worried for her.
One day at the pool with the kids, a friend of Bekah's who
was a nurse asked her whether I was abusive, and Bekah
had to think hard before answering, "Not physically."
Chaplain Bixler, our friends overseas, and those still at

Fort Carson all seemed to be waiting for me to come back to myself, praying for me and finding small ways to protect themselves from the person I had become.

For Mother's Day Bekah took a risk and asked me to come to church with her. We could go to an early service with light attendance, where they served gourmet coffee. If I could handle a Starbucks on a busy Saturday morning, she asked, perhaps I could handle a quiet church service with decent coffee? I still wasn't ready for crowds or for what I perceived as easy, untested assurances, but I knew it would mean a lot to her and I said I would go. I had preached at Walter Reed that past month about how we shouldn't neglect God. It had felt disingenuous as I felt like a stranger to God myself. I was going through the motions of a job, not a life's calling. Lately, church felt like a false environment to me. But I had not gone to church with my family since we'd been in Colorado and I felt I owed it to Bekah to go through the motions with my family as well.

The church wasn't far from our home. I was calm as we walked in, got our coffee, and milled about. But as soon as the crowd started to gather, the hypervigilance came back: a man's scratchy sweater, each dissonant note of the worship music, the sense that I could hear every conversation around me until it became deafening. All of the sudden I couldn't track the many stimuli surrounding me, and the familiar surge of adrenaline and fear shot up my spine. Bekah asked if I was all right. I said yes as we moved into the auditorium, thankful that she found us seats near the back.

During the service it was impossible for me to focus on the words and the singing. I was engulfed with anxiety. In a few minutes my only thought was *survival*, not grace or faith or God. This time it took just one look to Bekah. She understood when I left the church that I would be waiting outside.

When we got home I went out for a run. For now, my church was the outdoors and my prayer ritual was to run as fast as I could, to let the adrenaline of bliss replace the adrenaline of fear. It was during those quiet times that I could observe God's creation, could appreciate his work. In years past it was the Bible or prayer that brought me to a meditative state; now I had an alternate route to try to commune with God, a running trail.

▲▲▲

THINGS STARTED TO change around the time my father came to visit that May.

The night before he arrived, Bekah was making dinner and dropped some uncooked spaghetti on the floor. When she bent down to pick it up, a muscle twisted in her lower back and she froze in pain. Stuck in place, she sent Blaine to the front yard to find me. I was on the phone and told him I'd be right in. When Bekah started to cry, she sent Blaine out to try again, still half-expecting me to ignore her request for help.

I got off the phone and went inside. Seeing her in pain, with tears in her eyes, I was flooded with compassion for her. We had built up so many defenses around ourselves that it was easy to forget how human we both were, how easily we could be hurt. I tried to get her to the couch but she couldn't bear the pain, so I laid her on the floor. Was there anything I could do for her? I asked. I realized it was the first time I had asked that question in a long time, and I could see the relief fill Bekah's face. She asked me to help her stretch a little, so I pulled gently on her arms and legs to see if the kinks might roll out and tried to massage her back, tender and careful, like a husband should care for his wife.

For the rest of the night, I took over running the house. I made dinner, checked Tyler's blood levels before and after we ate, brought Bekah pain medication, and figured out what we'd do with my father the next morning. Bekah looked at me like a stranger who had shown up suddenly and might as quickly disappear; it had been so long since I'd behaved like a responsible adult.

The next morning Bekah still couldn't get out of bed. I hugged her and brought her breakfast. "I'll take care of everything," I told her.

The trip with my father turned out to be a simple visit: golf (I taught him how to hit the ball), Starbucks, playing with the boys. There were no deep conversations or difficult themes, just the wonderful relief of small talk. I couldn't believe that I handled it alone, without any fights. Perhaps I was able to function because I simply had no other choice. Bekah was always the one to save us at the last minute, and this time she couldn't move. I realized I had been leaning on her too much, thinking her resiliency was unending and focusing only on my own human limitations.

All the while Bekah stayed in bed and healed. It was her turn to hide out upstairs. And for the first time since I'd been home, I was able to look beyond myself and feel how much my family needed me.

17

▲▲▲

G R A C E

Spring 2007
I am trying to conduct self-care in the form of running and
playing golf. I find these sports to be a "spiritual" exercise
where I can be alone with God. I can meditate on Him
without saying or speaking words.

I WALKED INTO the Malogne House and John, a twenty-year-old soldier, spotted me from across the lobby. He had lost all movement in his right leg after an IED blast. While speaking with him once before I had learned that John was a devout Christian, though I knew little else about his personal life. I knew he had been diagnosed with PTSD, yet in our first talk he had seemed upbeat. As he walked toward me, I feared he wanted to talk about faith. On that topic I was still vulnerable, so unsure of my own grounding that another's firm belief made me uncomfortable.

"Hi there, John," I said, pulling myself together.

"Hi, Chaplain."

"I saw you at lunch with your mother. Did you enjoy the choir?" A high school choir had performed that day in the dining hall.

"Oh yeah, I like things like that . . . they help to calm me down."

"Calm you down?" I asked. Perhaps he wasn't doing as well as when I had seen him last.

"My equilibrium, my temper; I just want to"—he puts his arms around his throat as if strangling himself—"but I would never do that."

It seemed his confidence had subsided. Somehow the fact that he also felt weary helped me to relax and not worry about him judging me.

"You've been feeling a lot of anger?" I asked. I was surprised he was opening up, after our last, rather superficial conversation.

"Oh man, yes. But my mother is helping me. And my psychologist. And I'm real close with God. I talk to him every day."

"Really?" I realized I didn't feel bad upon hearing this. Hearing about His presence and grace with others, to my surprise, felt good, even if I wasn't the one in such close communion.

"Without Him I'd be in trouble. He helps me every day." It was so simple how he said it, so easy. Here I was—the chaplain—and John, who had been injured at such a young age, was the one in peaceful conversation with God.

When I looked down at his name tag, though, I realized I had screwed up. His name was Jim, not John. Disgust started to boil inside of me. This never would have happened to me before. Was I still so caught up in my own problems that I couldn't get a soldier's name right, even when I had counseled him before and his name tag was staring me right in the face? I was about to go into a downward spiral when I did what had become so difficult for me: I allowed for God's grace.

I hadn't always thought that there was such a thing as a perfect chaplain. But over the course of my deployments I had fallen for the praise; the accolades and awards fooled me into believing that I had reached the pinnacle of my profession—that if I made a mistake, I was failing to do my job. At that moment, looking at Jim, my journey from servant of God to a prideful chaplain became all too clear.

Perhaps I could attempt to care for others while I was still wounded. But to do that I'd need to get better at seeing past my own troubles to recognize and respect the suffering of others. Looking at Jim I realized that if he saw my weaknesses, maybe that would be just fine.

"So what does it mean, for you, to be close to God, *Jim*?" I smiled and he wordlessly accepted my correction.

"I feel blessed. Look, I have some control over my leg now." He pulled up his uniform to show me his disfigured leg. There was a large, pink lump where the wound was healing after what must have been several skin grafts and surgeries.

"The doctors told me I'd have to use a brace for the rest of my life. And I said to them. . . . 'you all just watch me.' " He turned and walked a few steps with his back to me, to illustrate that he would walk away from any doctor who told him he'd need a brace.

"You have an exceptional attitude."

"Why wouldn't I? I have my family. It doesn't matter if I don't have an expensive house or an expensive car. I have Wal-Mart clothes, man, three Big Dog shirts for fifteen dollars. I'm set."

"So relationships are what matter most in life?" I asked, trying to follow his discussion.

"They're the only thing that can really make us happy."

"You may be right." That had always been my theory about my life; how had I lost sight of it for so long?

▲▲▲

MORE THAN ONCE lately I found myself repeating a very short prayer: "Lord, I do not have much of a desire to serve you. Please give it to me." I had always been fascinated by Mark 9:17–24 when Jesus tells a man that everything is possible for him who believes. The man responds, in the same breath, "I do believe; help me overcome my unbelief." It's easy to forget that faith can be strong and fragile at the same time.

I had more than one person tell me that God was having me go through all of this so I could help others. At first I hated that line. God was allowing me and my family to go through this hell so that I could help others go through their hell? But at the same time maybe there was some truth to it; it was just hard to see at the time. What I knew was that now I would no longer put all my difficult questions into a "mystery cup." I was going to keep thinking and talking about them.

Yet I was also beginning to understand why so many vets either didn't talk about the wars they fought in or spoke out violently against them.

When I first enlisted as a soldier, in 1991, I wanted to go to war; I saw it as the greatest form of service to one's country. It took two deployments for me to recognize that violence simply leads to more violence, that we are poorly equipped as humans to judge who should deserve to die. I hate war. I've seen the spilled blood and the aftermath that soldiers and their families must face for the rest of their lives. It was my job as a chaplain to wade through that aftermath, to try to help them wash away a helplessness that threatened to permanently stain any normal person's consciousness.

I was realizing that it wasn't in my power to fight the realities of war. But, in seeking grace for myself, I recognized that I did what I could with the resources at hand, as did all those around me. I'm proud of my service and the service of all the soldiers but not of how the war was handled from above.

Anger about the war had made it harder for me to talk with soldiers and to talk with God, who I had pushed away for so long. But slowly, in flashes, I was starting to remember the peace I had once known in communion with Him. I missed God, and I was lonely.

I knew that God would restore our relationship if I

sought in earnest to seek Him. One night, in the quiet of my living room when everyone was asleep, I opened the Bible and sat on my knees silently pleading for grace, praying to God to break through my many layers of pride, praying for more of what I had felt that day in the on-call room after the biggest wake-up call of my career. I wanted to hold on to this need. I needed grace and I needed to give others grace. I understood I was never going to be the perfect chaplain I'd hoped to be; I was going to be the chaplain God needed me to be.

People were praying for me, Bekah and her family first and foremost. Her sister-in-law Rose, who was on medication for postpartum depression, e-mailed me and shared her own fears; when she told me she was praying for me, I actually felt it. So I prayed for her. Although many of the soldiers I counseled those weeks appeared to have more trust in God than I could muster, I began to feel enveloped in prayer and less ashamed in their presence. I abandoned the idea of being the religious expert, a notion that had been with me since I joined the army Chaplaincy, and instead saw myself returning to a simple equation I had found in my early days as a hospital chaplain—the patients could learn from me and I could learn from them in spite of our failings. Day by day, I could feel God refining me.

Sitting at my desk one morning I opened my leather-bound Bible to 2 Corinthians 12:9–10 where the Apostle Paul speaks:

But He said to me, "My grace is sufficient for you, for my power is made perfect in weakness." Therefore

I will boast all the more gladly about my weaknesses, so that Christ's power may rest on me. That is why, for Christ's sake, I delight in weaknesses, in insults, in hardships, in persecutions, in difficulties. For when I am weak, then I am strong.

18

▲▲▲

W O U N D E D   H E A L E R

Memorial Day 2007

My heart is heavy with sadness for all the lives lost, all the lives sacrificed. I have felt the anguish of watching a trooper be killed-in-action on the battlefield. If someone could have weighed in to assist in that exact second before death, that person would be here today. But that was not the case. I would like to believe that I have ultimate control over my life situation, but I am sadly reminded, more often than I would like, that I do not. Some will look at me and say, "He was a caring man who tried to help others." Others will say, "He had too many problems and wasted his life."

Right now, I look at what I have done and I want to say that I had a positive effect on some. I'm not sure though, I was so busy "doing" that "being" had little place in my life. I gave 100% of myself to my soldiers and I cannot think of any more that I could have done. I did the best I could do with what I had. But why am I so down? Why do I feel more depressed the more I write? Dr. Currie told me, during my time at Coatesville, that when you care about what you do in life, you are bound to be affected. This made a lot of sense to me in the moment and as I continue to reflect, it makes that much more sense. I cared about my soldiers! As my eyes tear up, I can honestly say that I hurt because they were injured and killed.

I look at life with a different perspective than before the deployments. The colors that surround me are brighter. The old wooden structure across from me as I sit in Starbucks is dilapidated. The aged rusted metal roof sits strongly attached to the structure and yet the siding is missing. The Sheetrock flaps with every lick of the wind and yet the wooden picket fence is unaffected.

The grass is so green and the leaves on the trees gracefully oscillate with the wind. Why did it take nearly getting killed to notice this wonderful creation around me? How could I be so blind to what stood in front of my face? My soldiers and those in the Regiment that were killed lost the ability to appreciate what I now hold dear to me.

Why must some suffer this paralyzing grief and others escape it and never even know that such a feeling exists? I don't know. It is one of those mysteries that remain with God. So many mysteries have filled this cup that it seems to overflow. How can I say that God protected me the day I could have been killed by a sniper as I talked with the platoon sergeant in a M1A2 Abrams Battle Tank with a total lack of caution? How can I say this when Lugo was killed the following day in the same exact tank, location, and position in the tank? How can I say this when the following day another soldier was lost? Does God love me more than them? I don't think so! Every creation is loved by God and not knowing why some die and others do not escapes me. "It rains on the just and the unjust" echoes in my mind; it is almost deafening! Can someone look at the situation I described above and say that God protected me? Not them? I would not say that! I am speechless, trying to make sense of the senseless.

LEAVING ARMY MINISTRY might have helped me—soldiers were a constant trigger of my trauma—but it would also have meant running away, from God and from ministry. So I decided to remain in the chaplaincy. Running away from God doesn't work. I had tried.

I thought often of the story of Jonah, who runs away when God tells him to deliver a stern warning to his enemies, the warmongering Assyrians of Nineveh (which, coincidentally, is where modern day Mosul and Tal Afar are situated). Jonah rebels at the idea of being a pawn of God but when he finds himself in the belly of a whale, he repents and gains God's mercy. Yet he still must deliver God's message, and when his enemies are granted that same forgiveness, he is angered. He wanted God to be inconsistent in his grace.

Jonah's is a story about the frailty of humans and the power of God, about a confused being who runs away from God yet also struggles to be a servant of God. There is no perfect ending to the story of Jonah, but we know lessons were learned, and I'd like to think his faith was deepened, not diminished.

My time at Coatesville hadn't cured me, there was no

perfect ending to my treatment. I was still in need of help, but I was also ready to begin moving forward and healing, not alone anymore, but with God's grace to guide me.

More and more soldiers came home from the war each day with traumatic brain injuries, lost limbs, and broken lives. It was impossible for me to counsel as many soldiers as I had in the past. In Iraq there were days when I counseled dozens and led ceremonies for hundreds. Before Coatesville I might easily have seen as many as fifteen a day. Now I met with no more than four or five soldiers each day.

One night I was dozing in the chaplain sleep room when my pager went off. I took a deep breath and dialed the number on the screen. There was no Code Blue, no cardiac arrest, and no risk of death. Instead, a nurse at the Intensive Care Unit told me there was a spat between an in-law and the wife of an injured soldier. She needed me to negotiate.

When I reached the ICU, the nurse led me to the soldier's room, which was dark and crowded with medical equipment. My heart dropped when I saw him. His face was disfigured with swelling and his body twisted in pain despite the fact that he appeared heavily drugged. A tube ran down his throat and every few minutes he seemed to try to tug it out of his mouth. His wife stood at the left of his bed, holding his hand. Both appeared to be in their thirties. The soldier had kicked off his blankets, and lay exposed in a flimsy hospital gown. The mother was nowhere in sight.

The wife looked as if she had been loyally by his side

for some time—her hair hadn't been washed in days and her clothes, blue jeans and a brown T-shirt, were wrinkled and sweat soaked. Her face was tight with stress.

I stood at the foot of the bed and asked her what was troubling her. She told me that she thought she was losing her mind. She and her toddler as well as her father-in-law and his wife were all living in the same single room at Malogne House. The parents were not on orders to be at Walter Reed and so they had no free housing of their own. The wife and baby slept on one bed; her husband's parents on another. She had no escape, no solitude.

The arguing was nonstop. Even during visiting hours they were on top of one another. That evening everyone had been in the ICU room and the tension boiled over; a shoving match had started.

I walked out to talk with the nurse manager. The soldier had been diagnosed with Traumatic Brain Injury, one of the signature injuries of the war in Iraq. When an IED explodes, it sets off blast waves that can rip through brain tissue, the effects of which could emerge weeks or months after the incident. This soldier was one of a growing number who suffered this terrible fate.

Lost in all this was his wife—distraught about her husband, raising a toddler alone, surrounded by terrified parents. We brought the wife into the ICU unit's break room and hammered out separate visiting hours for the family. I told her I would start work on getting the in-laws orders for a separate hotel room, and within a week or so—with the help of the Malogne House staff and others—we were able to get the parents housed separately even without orders. The members of this family each had a bed of their own, and it made all the difference in the world.

I may have been carrying a lighter caseload, but soon realized the benefits were tremendous: I was becoming a better listener. Sometimes it was all I could do to find someone a pillow to lay their head on. I rediscovered that pastoral care takes many forms. Small acts are sacred.

▲▲▲

ONE DAY I walked into the Malogne House's small dining room for lunch. Sitting alone and watching television was a young soldier with his foot propped up on a nearby chair. Like everyone does at Walter Reed, I quickly tried to guess his injury—perhaps an IED blast to his arms. I hadn't met him before and knew nothing about him, except that it was possible he just wanted to be left alone to watch TV.

"Hi, I'm Chaplain Benimoff."

He looked up at me "Hi, Sir. I'm Carlos Velasquez." We shook hands.

I turned my eyes to the TV.

"What are you watching?"

"I don't know, Sir. I hate these shows." He turned away from the TV, so I asked him whether he'd mind if I sat down. He didn't.

"Do you mind if we chat a little?"

"That's fine," he replied, finishing off a milk shake.

"Do you mind if I just call you Carlos?"

"Not at all, Sir."

"Are you in med hold?" I asked. He was. Medical Hold is transition phase when the Army determines if a soldier can go back to duty or needs to be medically discharged. Being on medical hold meant that he was still on active duty, for now.

"Well, I'm one of the med hold chaplains and I am trying to meet everyone. So how long have you been here?"

"Since March, I want to get out of here. I start my med board next month." It was now the end of May, he had been here six months already.

"You seem excited."

"Oh, yes, Sir. I hate it here."

"How so?"

"You know, my squad leader gives me a hard time. I'm not allowed to go to my appointments in PTs even though I can under the hospital policy." He was wearing his army uniform instead of the more comfortable PTs— black shorts and a gray army T-shirt.

"And the physical therapists have techs under them that take care of four patients at a time so I don't get any one-on-one. I stopped going and I do the therapy by myself." I imagined him struggling through his physical therapy, doing it alone in the solace of his own room.

"Do you mind me asking what brought you here?"

"IED," Carlos pointed to his arm.

"My God . . . what happened?"

"We were driving in a convoy when I got hit. I knew

something wasn't right that day. We normally traveled on the other side of the road. I heard a big blast and the next thing you know we were hit. I crawled on top of the Hummer and I saw the driver, Mills. He lost both legs."

I tried to keep my mind focused but it flashed to a soldier from one of my deployments who had lost his leg. I kept picturing him and all I could say to Carlos was, "Wow, that must have been terrible." But in a moment my thoughts went back to Carlos. I was getting better at staying focused on others, not myself.

"The guys were carrying me and I told them to go help Mills."

"Do you have flashbacks?"

"No." It sounded like an automated response.

"I'm not asking because I am going to report what you are saying to your COC [Chain of Command]. I'm asking because I know that when my guys came back, they had similar issues. I had similar issues, I'm still fighting them."

"Really? You okay?"

"Yes, I think I'm getting there."

"You know, I grew up in the ghetto. When I was a kid, I heard gunshots all the time, I had bullets whizzing by my head. I've seen someone cut in half by a Samurai sword. So when I heard gun shots in Iraq, I didn't react too much, I just said to myself, 'Bullets again.' But the IED blast was loud. That was different."

"Yeah, I would think so." I found myself suddenly curious about whether he was connected to his faith, and inquired.

"My parents were Catholic. I was thinking about going back to the church, haven't been since I was little."

"Why go back now?"

"I could have died. I was very lucky. Why me? Why did I get lucky? I want to know. I also want to go back for my boy. He's two. I wasn't too good as a kid and I want better for my son."

"What's his name?"

"It's also Carlos." He smiled. "I go home every weekend so he is more comfortable with me. At first he didn't want me touching him."

"Yeah, that was the same with my youngest after my first deployment," I told him.

We talked some more—about how he wanted to buy a motorcycle, and how his two-year-old loved women's breasts (like father like son maybe, I joked, and we both split up laughing).

I respected Carlos because he was willing to look for help. I hoped he would connect with God and that the relationship would be life sustaining, going beyond the occasional church visit.

For him, an IED blast was reorienting his life. For me, it was two tours in Iraq. I hoped, for both our sakes, it was for the better and that God was giving us both a fresh start.

When we wrapped it up, I told him I would be there for him if he wanted to talk further. I told him "I have heard your sacred story"—that I had really listened.

▲▲▲

Rebekah Benimoff, June 2007
A month to move . . . somewhere? Who knows where!
"Trust me with the details," says the Lord, "Pray and turn
your concerns over to me, and trust." Again I am struck by
the fact that faith is a choice.

In June we found out that my next assignment would be
Fort Sam Houston in San Antonio, Texas. I would be a
chaplain for the Army's largest battalion—a population of
three thousand soldiers training to be combat medics. It
was a huge assignment and I could only pray I'd be up for
it. I would be a caregiver, in other words, to a battalion of
caregivers.

We'd have to move once again, which was especially
hard on Bekah. She had finally made some friends and
was finding her own voice by leading a Bible study group.
Neither of us was ready for the move, but I brought the
laptop down from my office upstairs and we sat close to
each other on the couch to research house listings. There
was nothing available on post, but the Army would pay
up to $1,300 per month for our housing costs, so we
spent our nights on the couch scouring the web, listening
to each other's hopes for a new home. I wanted a private
computer room and she agreed that I needed a place to
unwind and gather myself. She wanted a large kitchen
since our families lived near San Antonio and she wanted
to hold big dinners. She also wanted all the bedrooms
close together, in case Tyler had any late-night emergen-
cies. I made her concerns the deal breaker in the home
search and when we found the perfect home, it was

almost disappointing that our joint mission was over. So we began watching movies, anything to keep us close on the couch together.

One night an old '70s movie, *Heaven Can Wait*, was on TV; it was the first movie Bekah and I had ever seen together, back when we first started dating in college.

This time the final locker-room scene choked me up like it never had before. A dead quarterback has been given a fleeting, second chance at life to play with his team. For me the movie was about camaraderie and loss. At the end of the film, the quarterback's past, his accomplishments, his relationships, the sum of who he was—it was all lost—he'd never regain the life and the friends he had. I had spent months, if not almost a year, as a stranger to my wife, but at that moment I finally broke down in front of her. She hugged me and listened. The only thing she asked was, "Who are you missing?" The soldiers I had known had paid the ultimate sacrifice and would soon be forgotten. Their families would remember them, but even so, memories become blurry. All that they were, all that made them unique, their idiosyncrasies would be swallowed up by time. Even I, who had known these soldiers and in some cases written their memorial ceremonies, was now trying to change and reframe my memory of them, to dim the small, disturbing details of our time in Iraq.

Rebekah Benimoff, Late June 2007
Praying for Roger really helped me to step out of the struggle to "be" with him, as well as the resentful attitude. I was able to set aside my own hurt and empathize with what

Roger was going through, as well as pray for him. I under-
stood what Jesus meant when He said, "love your enemies,
and pray for those who persecute you." It is difficult to hate
someone when you are praying for them. When I would
pray for Roger, I would be filled with a love and compassion
for Him that came from God, and was not of myself. I put
my "self" aside—my selfishness, my grudges, my pain, and
looked to the needs of another. I saw Roger as hurting, too.
Something that is hard to see when the person is taking that
hurt out on you. It was easy to see the many offenses I had
against Roger. It was not always so easy to see the pain he
had which was causing the offense. When I prayed for
Roger, God filled me with compassion for him and I could
get a glimpse of how much pain he was in. And in those mo-
ments I loved him in a way I had not loved him for quite
some time.

19

COMMUNION

THERE WAS A prayer I thought of often, one I had used when standing in the Iraqi sands with soldiers who had just survived an attack, but had lost friends who weren't so lucky. Psalm 121:1–8: "My help comes from the LORD, the Maker of heaven and earth. He will not let your foot slip—he who watches over you will not slumber. . . ."

But my foot had slipped. Some may blame my crisis of faith on PTSD, but that's too easy. Faith is something, by its very nature, that should be tested. I had thought that if there was a test, it would come in Iraq, a world of blood and tears, lost friends, near misses, and body after body shipped home in cheap wooden caskets. The fault lines started appearing there, but I didn't crack. There was no time to think and too much adrenaline. My problems happened after I got home, to our warm house here on this cul-de-sac, surrounded by my wife and my boys and the ever-present sound, not of guns, but of the neighborhood kids playing outside our front door. War zones have a way of traveling home with you.

I think of Army Specialist Brent Hendrix, a twenty-two-year old who lost his right leg and broke his jaw when his Stryker vehicle hit an IED in Rawah, Iraq. Recovering at Malogne House he told me how his Southern Baptist faith pulled him through. "Yes, there are the Ten Commandments and we know 'Thou shalt not kill.' But when they're shooting at you, there's not much else you can think about." He says he wasn't afraid of death. "I'm good with God. I was ready for him whenever he wanted to take me. My doctor said I should have died four times over. I talked to God a lot more while I was over there—I told him, 'You can take me any day, I'm still with you." Other soldiers felt differently. When I sat outside Malogne House with National Guard Specialist George Schmidt, who was raised as a Methodist but became a Wiccan. He was taking a break from treatment for PTSD and bipolar anxiety. He told me that during his deployment to Ramadi there was no middle ground when it came to faith. "Either you're running to God, grasping to hold on to the guy you were before you came to Iraq, or you're running right away from him because of what you're seeing." Then there was the Army Specialist who was being treated for PTSD after two deployments. He was Catholic, but that was before Iraq. "I haven't gotten it back since. Once you get there you wonder how God could allow anyone to go through that. The second deployment was even worse." Or the Army Sergeant who was raised Catholic but wasn't a believer. The Sergeant had his first hints of faith when he lost a chunk of his right heel in an IED blast in Baghdad. "I was lying in the hospital in Germany and a chaplain walked in and handed me a necklace with a medallion of a saint. The chaplain told me 'You're alive. God must have a plan for you.' And for a brief period I believed that might just be true. I should have died. The IED exploded right under me."

Late Spring 2007
"I waited patiently for the LORD; *he turned to me and heard my cry. He lifted me out of the slimy pit, out of the mud and mire; he set my feet on a rock and gave me a firm place to stand." Psalm 40:1–3*

   The essence of this verse is that the Lord is faithful and waits for his children, i.e. me. He stands by willing to assist me and waits patiently as I deal with my thoughts and feelings from the deployments. Anger, sadness, dismay, and grief are a few of my feelings that are still very present in my life today. I cannot tie a pretty bow on my story and I don't believe that God would want me to. Drawing a balance between my intense feelings and God's assistance in my life is more of where I am presently at. I could not have come to this place in my life without God's active presence in my life. He gave me room to "cry out" as I flashbacked to traumatic events and the many soldiers that my unit lost in the two deployments to Iraq. He allowed me to slowly move through the "mud and mire." And he is assisting me in a new chapter of my life to have a transformed foundation to stand upon. I still think about the soldiers today and the lives

*that were suddenly changed due to circumstances beyond our
control. They will forever be with me in memory and my
prayer is that this scripture, the Lord's faithfulness, would
be meaningful and helpful to them.*

Any truly difficult time is a war zone—a divorce, the
loss of a child, an illness—the emotional violence is the
same. In Iraq I once quoted from Hebrews in my journal,
"What is faith? It is the confident assurance that what we
hope for is going to happen." But maybe that's not quite
it. Maybe it's the confident assurance that, even if you
don't always get what you're hoping for, you won't be
alone.

▲▲▲

IT WAS A muggy day and I was doing my rounds behind
Malogne House when I ran into Evan, a double amputee
in his early twenties who lost both his arms above the
elbow from an IED.

I had met Evan a month earlier, when he first came
out of the hospital. According to his charts he was suffering from it all—insomnia, depression, PTSD, nightmares, flashbacks, and, more simply, failed expectations.
In our initial meeting he, like many recently injured soldiers, made it a point of pride to be upbeat.

When I saw him again, he was sitting on a bench next
to two women. As I moved closer I realized he looked
different than he had before—depressed and tired. He
was wearing a T-shirt and had grown a beard. He had

bandages over the stumps of his arms, and it was obvious he wasn't doing well.

One of the women next to him was in her sixties, dressed in red; the other was in her thirties and had crutches propped next to her.

"Do you mind if I join you?"

They all welcomed me.

I patted Evan on the back and joked, "This is one of my soldiers, one of my flock." Everyone laughed and I introduced myself to the women. One of them was his mother, the other was a fellow patient. It was hot and humid and although we sat under a tree, the shade provided little relief.

When I asked Evan how he was doing, he just said "All right" as he stared down at the grass. His words were incongruent with his nonverbal cues, as we say in counseling, so I decided to test them.

"So what's wrong?" I looked straight at him.

He moved his head up to look at me. "I don't know . . . I can't sleep and I'm not getting better. I've been here six months."

The mother jumped in, "You can't be too hard on yourself." I kept my eyes on Evan, wishing he had been able to finish his answer.

"Yeah," was all Evan replied.

"What's going on with your arms?" I asked, making a point to say "arms."

"They won't heal. And, I'm having another surgery." He seemed profoundly exhausted.

Now the woman with the crutches chimed in. "I was

too hard on myself and I ran too soon. The next day I was in the emergency room."

The women were trying to make him feel better, but in fact they weren't allowing him to talk.

"Evan, I can see why you're down. That makes a lot of sense," I said. He was looking at me now. "It sounds like you expected to have your arms by now."

"Most of the people that came here with me have theirs." He looked to the ground again and stomped out his cigarette. I could almost feel his despair in the muggy air around him.

"Just the other day I saw a guy who didn't have his arms yet," said one of the women.

I did my best to stay professional and focused on Evan, who couldn't get a word in edgewise.

"I think he is talking about the soldiers who got here the same time he did," I told the women. Evan nodded his head in agreement.

"Well, they might have had fewer injuries." She tried again to help.

"No, some of them had worse injuries," Evan responded flatly.

"So, what's happening with your injuries now?" I asked, trying to give him space to talk about his concerns.

"I have open sores."

"That's why they can't give you prosthetics yet, right?"

"Yup. One of my stitches didn't dissolve and they had to open up the scab and take it out. I'm on blood thinners so it takes a long time to develop scabs."

"It's not your fault that this is happening," offered his mother.

"You said you weren't sleeping?" I asked.

"I wake up every hour from my nightmares, so I'm wiped during the day."

"You just have to look at the good things, the beautiful things all around us," offered the mom. "Remember that butterfly we saw yesterday?" I broke protocol a bit and turned to Evan to get his reaction to the butterfly.

"Did that help?"

"No." He laughed.

"I guess it is hard to see the good things when you are living every moment with the bad things?"

He looked up at me with interest, even a little energy in his voice. "Yes."

"Maybe keeping busy would help?" Again his mother was trying to help, but her method was avoidance of his pain, and it seemed to be pushing Evan deeper into a place where he was alone and misunderstood. I felt like I understood him as he detached. I looked to the mother.

"You see, part of this is education. With PTSD, you just can't forget the bad things or pretend they are not there. That doesn't work." Evan watched me closely. "Forging through the difficult feelings actually helps the person in the healing process." That is the theory. That's why we talked, went through Critical Stress Debriefing Incidents, and did our best not to push things under the rug. But who can really say what's the best method; each person is so unique. At that moment, I just hoped it resonated with Evan.

A group of soldiers walked up and started chatting

with us, looking for a place to smoke on the benches. The soldiers were all from the cavalry, so it felt like I was among family as we made small talk. I relaxed, and Evan also seemed better. I got up to leave.

"Okay, I have to go, guys, but I'll be back later; I'm on late duty today."

"Sir, do you know what room I'm in?" asked Evan.

"No, which is it?"

He gave me the number and then asked if I had a business card with my numbers.

"No, I'm not that important, but I'll write them down for you."

I found an index card in my shirt pocket and wrote out my details for him, so touched that he wanted my help, so thankful that he'd be there for me to talk to as well.

We met again four times, on the benches by the pond, in his room, in the lobby.

I just listened to him. He was struggling to survive a new life he hadn't bargained for. His words and tragic second-guessing echoed those of so many hospital patients, soldiers, and others I had counseled over the years, even my own words: "If only I had waited a few seconds more to turn that corner" or "I just don't understand why I can't stop this."

His sores were not healing and he wasn't able to get prosthetics and begin the process of living as an independent person. Soldiers who had lost their limbs at the same time were now walking right past him. Even I would leave Walter Reed before he could. During one of our last talks, he asked me why this had happened to him.

I didn't think his question was so much directed at me but at the world at large.

Why?

Yes, he had gone to Iraq to serve his country and had been an unlucky statistic in an unlucky situation. We both understood that. He still had faith that his arms would somehow, must somehow improve. But grief is a masterful interrogator.

Why?

"I don't know," I told him, looking into his eyes. We were silent after that. I can only hope he understood that while I didn't have an answer, it was only because I so fundamentally understood the question.

Much like a Psalm in the Old Testament, *Faith Under Fire* is my "Psalm of Lament." It spans three years of my deployment as an Army Captain, my return to the United States, and my slow and painful return to a new and better relationship with my family and with God. I wrote about what I saw and what my soldiers lived through: helicopter crashes, suicide bombings, and the spiritual and—all too often—marital troubles of the men and women I counseled. My journal entries were penned during the quiet moments I was able to steal between my rounds as a chaplain in Tal Afar and at Walter Reed. I'm supposed to be a spiritual guide for soldiers, yet my time in Iraq brought me to the lowest depths of confusion and despair. There seemed to be no way to reconcile a loving God with a God who would allow the suffering I witnessed.

Take away the bloodshed and the guns and my struggle is much like that of others—of all walks of life and beliefs, whether of a religious nature or not—who are simply trying to understand a world in which there is so much pain and suffering. It often seems ours is a world where faith and justice fade into the distance when they are needed most. Yet faith is something that by its very nature will be tested, and coming to grips with our feelings will determine the extent of healing in our lives.

What is unique about my journey—from a rock solid faith, to the threat of losing it, and to a renewed relationship with

God—is that it was accelerated. It's a simple truth: Life is accelerated in a war zone. For two years it felt as if my life was stuck on fast-forward with God appearing as a spectator, not responding to my desperate calls for him to hit the pause button. What happens to us when we face the worst that life has to throw at us? What happens when time seems to stand still, when we are able to see our fallibility pass before our very eyes, we are able to hear and memorize every sound that surrounds us, and we can smell those unforgettable scents that will never escape our memories? These thoughts and feelings are branded into us and then it is our job to try to make sense of what can often feel senseless.

Now that I've passed through the lowest valleys of my life, I find that the beauty of faith is that throughout my crisis I still cried out to God. I've journeyed through the heights and depths of spirituality and I was forced to ask the big questions of life and seek its meaning in ways I wasn't able to grasp before.

At times it's been hard to imagine sharing my story; I never expected to write a book. But when the letters poured in after *Newsweek* published an article on May 7, 2007, about army chaplains that featured my story and journal entries, I quickly discovered that there are many people who also have suffered emotional and spiritual wounds. I became convinced that my story, expanded into book form, would touch anyone who had questions about their beliefs, whether those beliefs are religious or simply deeply held views on how the world works, and whether they had served in a war zone or not. After all, most trauma can make a person *feel* like she or he is in a war zone—ask anyone who has survived a violent crime, been a victim of abuse, lost a child, or been profoundly hurt by a relationship. My experience is only unique in that it all happened so quickly and against a backdrop of extreme violence and constant loss.

My hope is that after reading the book, you will be motivated to explore your own histories, traumas, and beliefs, and recognize the inherent parallels between my experience and yours. It's easy not to question and it's easy to suppress your fears, yet we all need to understand ourselves more deeply and often need a catalyst to do so. This is my story: a working chaplain who struggled through the depths of my faith, confronted his humanity, cried out to God, and allowed his faith to be refined.

I'll never forget ministering to a group of soldiers at Walter Reed when a wounded soldier held my *Newsweek* article in his hand and he said, "Chaplain, I read your article and now I have permission to grieve."

Blessings,
Roger Benimoff

I want to thank God, above all. From my birth, your hands protected, molded, and nurtured me. Your eternal patience and love served as a stabilizing force in my life, and I especially want to thank you for allowing me to explore my thoughts and emotions freely and openly. You have always allowed me to be where I needed to be spiritually and emotionally, and I am honored to be your "hands and feet" in the world.

I cannot thank my devoted wife, Rebekah, enough for her steady love and support. Your contribution, not only to our marriage and family, but also to this book, has been invaluable. Your relationship with God has been unshakable, and God knew exactly what he was doing when he brought us together. You have always stood by my side, even as we disagreed, and I love you. Thank you for being you.

Tyler and Blaine, I thank God for you every day. My hope is that this book will help you to know a little more about me and assist you in your future endeavors. I cannot think of a better legacy of faith to leave you with, and I pray that you would put God first in your lives. I love you both.

I want to thank my family—the Benimoffs, Yurkiewiczes, Ledermans, and the McIntyres. You have been there for me in times of joy and in times of grief. As my theology has blossomed, I have come to the conclusion that relationships are at the center of a meaningful life. Your relationship with me has been a great source of encouragement. Mom, you have always stuck by my side, believed in me, and I love you. Uncle Jack, thank you for the endless supply of Starbucks! Ernie and Liz, we couldn't have made it this far without your love, support, and prayers.

Thank you, Eve. It has been quite a journey, beginning with the *Newsweek* article and now the book. I still don't know how you did it—*Newsweek*, Ben, the challenges and surprises along the way, and the book! I admire your writer's touch and I am forever in your debt. Rebekah and I could not have done this without you.

Thank you to Mary Choteborsky at Crown for deciding my story should be written and that you would make that happen, and to our agent, Alice Martell, for her wisdom and encouragement from day one.

I want to thank everyone who contributed to the book who profoundly shaped my experience in Iraq and after. Specifically, Rebekah Benimoff, Tyler Benimoff, Blaine Benimoff, H.R. McMaster, Christopher Hickey, Geoff Bailey, David Causey, James Bixler, Ryan Howell, Renee Howell, Freddy Serrano, John Wilwerding, Maria Kimble, Andrew Seng, Rose McIntyre, and Uncle Jack. Your contribution has added a dimension of life that could not be had otherwise.

To Ryan and Freddy—it has been quite a journey! I'm honored you let me into your lives and thank you for allowing me to be your pastor and friend. I am a better person because of it.

Thanks, Geoff! We have shared a lot of great memories, humorous moments, and along the way, I think we have taught each other a little bit about tact. Thanks for always sticking by my side and pulling up the slack. Your prayers, concern, and friendship are continuing sources of strength.

To my care team at Walter Reed and Brooke Army Medical Center: Dr. Christopher Lang and Dr. Leslie Cooper, thank you. Dr. Cooper—I believe your magic wand had a delayed effect, but it took! Dr. Jillian Ballantyne, Linda Patterson, and Dr. Richard Poe—I will always appreciate your investment in me.

To my mentors: So many people have taken the time to nurture me throughout my life and I want to name a few. Doug Tipps, thank you for bringing humanity to the Gospel. Mickey Porter, thank you for investing countless hours in Rebekah and me throughout our college years. To my Army Endorser, Dr. George Pickle, your compassion and concern for me and my family has been a constant source of encouragement. I look forward to our continued journey. James Bixler, thank you for personally investing in me and I especially enjoyed our collaboration with EMDR and the LIFE process. Dave Deppmeier, thank you for taking me under your wing, investing your time and energy, and for your continued friendship. To my former CPE supervisors, Jay Perez, John Takacs, Mary Stewart Hall, Carole Somers-Clark, the late Mike Stein, Alvester Gales, and Richard Dayringer—your humanity and theology have left an indelible impact on me. You helped make it possible for me to explore my humanity and my theology, and I am forever grateful. Thank you for devoting countless hours to me; I can only hope to bless others as you have blessed me.

EVE CONANT'S

ACKNOWLEDGMENTS

I first met Roger Benimoff in the early spring of 2007. I was researching a story for *Newsweek* on what is known as "provider fatigue" among the military medics, psychologists, and mental health workers who care for the soldiers and vets of Iraq and Afghanistan. An army social worker by then serving in Afghanistan, Maria Kimble, told me she had a chaplain friend with a story to tell, if he was willing to tell it. I reached out to Roger but for more than a month he didn't return my e-mails. Later I would find out that Roger didn't respond because at that time he was an inpatient himself at the Coatesville Veteran's Administration facility.

My deadline came and went, but I was still curious about Roger. Eventually, with the gracious permission of the Walter Reed administration—which was in the midst of a national scandal over its care of veterans—we were able to talk. The Walter Reed representative who listened in on our interview spent most of it in tears, and I was also deeply moved. We all know that Iraq is a traumatic place. But what few of us have heard is how the Iraq war and its aftermath can affect the faith of those who serve.

Chaplains are meant to be anchors of faith in the turbulent seas of war. But we're all human. A 2006 U.S. military survey found that 27 percent of chaplains and their assistants in the field reported high levels of burnout, with similar results for military medics and mental health caregivers. This was hardly surprising—extended and repeat deployments, the 24/7 nature of serving in a war zone, and the death and casualty rates all combine to make Iraq a profoundly difficult place to serve. Like many soldiers I've interviewed over the years who've served in Iraq, Roger was proud of his service, but it took a toll.

The war in Iraq will, at some point, come to a close. When it does there will be tens of thousands of troops returning home, many of them with physical, emotional, and—in some cases—spiritual wounds. Spiritual doubt, after all, is one of the lesser-known symptoms of PTSD. If Vietnam is any guide, the consequences of the war in Iraq—as it continues and even after it ends—will remain an unresolved issue for the American psyche. Exploring, in-depth, how some individuals have coped with that return can only help the healing process.

I spoke with several chaplains who served in Iraq as part of what became a *Newsweek* cover story on Roger. Some said their faith was never shaken. Yet others told a different tale: one chaplain was so traumatized he had nightmares of throwing up flag-draped caskets. Another told me of laying 40-pound bags of ice on dead soldiers and conducting so many ramp ceremonies for the fallen that he had to wonder if God was really listening to his prayers.

What is unique about Roger, however, is that his Iraq experience both strained and strengthened his faith and that he made the effort to record that journey. In the midst of the chaos, he confided in his diary, a maroon, leather-bound collection of 126 unlined pages, telling the story of not just what he saw in Iraq, but what he saw in himself as his deployment progressed and as he struggled to stay afloat at Walter Reed.

▲▲▲

Roger, I want to thank you for your willingness to share your story, and in such painful detail. I know this hasn't always been easy. Bekah, the support you've shown Roger through this project has been profound. Even while handling two little boys and a husband still grappling with PTSD, you've found the courage to share intimate details of family life, your own journals, and your personal struggles.

I'd like to thank our wonderful editor at Crown, Mary Choteborsky, for seeing the potential in this story and taking the long hours to help bring it to fruition. You've poured your heart and your time into this project and have been an incredible source of support, much-needed critique, and encouragement. For our agent, Alice Martell, thank you for guiding us through the wilderness as we first started this endeavor. Your advice has been invaluable.

I'd also like to thank all those who contributed their memories of serving with Roger in Iraq and at Walter Reed—your voices added depth, detail, and perspective to this story, and we are so grateful. For certain details of the Tal Afar offensives I'm indebted to the embed reporting of Jonathan Finer from the *Washington Post* and Michael Ware from *Time*, whose work is quoted on page 110.

To my bureau chief, Jeff Bartholet, you lit the spark under this project and I can't thank you enough for that. To both you and Jon Meacham—thank you for giving me the time to pursue it. Alan Cullison, thank you for your encouragement, applying your wise editing skills to some of the earliest drafts of the book. Daniel Stone, thank you for the fact checking and the snacks, and Pat Wingert, thank you for your advice on books and life. To Mariana Ramirez and Ashley, I'm so grateful to you two for keeping my little Bennett happy during some of those long nights. Cathy Bean, I loved hearing your interpretation of grace. To Denis Sigman, thank you for all the encouragement over the past two years. Most of all, I'd like to thank my mother, Helena, for flying out and holding down the fort in all ways and for such an extended period. Your love and support, as always, carries me through.

1. What do you think are some of the reasons that compel people to travel to war zones when they go by choice (not drafted into service)? Have you ever been drawn to a dangerous situation out of choice? If so, why?

2. What did Roger do to spiritually prepare for his second combat deployment to Iraq? What are some ways you prepare, either psychologically or spiritually, for a difficult time?

3. How does a person care for him- or herself? What activities have worked for you? What techniques did Roger use during deployment? Do you think they were helpful?

4. Why did Roger emphasize the importance of being a "quiet presence" with his soldiers?

5. Why did Roger, as a college student, initially doubt his call to ministry? Do you remember some key moments of questioning in your life that helped lead you to your current profession or life role?

6. To prepare for his second deployment, Roger gathered supplies and resolidified his bond with his prayer group. What did he not anticipate? Have you had a similar experience of being unprepared for a journey? How so?

7. Do you think Roger's journaling helped or hindered his ability to deal with his emotions in Iraq? After he returned home? If you journal, do you feel that it helps you?

8. In chapter 5, Roger describes how he relied more on his clinical skills than on his faith. How did he use his faith, and how did he overlook his faith? Talk about an experience that you've had where you relied on yourself more than God.

9. How do you imagine Rebekah felt as she assisted her neighbors with the death of their loved ones? Secondary Post-Traumatic Stress Disorder is a term that explains how caregivers and others who have not had a direct experience of trauma can still be affected by it. Has there been a tragedy affecting others that surprised you in how much it affected you?

10. Both while he was serving, and after he came home, how were Rebekah's and Roger's challenges similar? How were they different? What role did God play for each of them?

11. Rebekah and Roger's relationship was extremely strained when he returned home, more than when he was in Iraq. What brought the couple back together?

12. Can you think of a time when you and a loved one faced a crisis? How did you react similarly; how did you respond differently?

13. Rebekah journaled about her faith and her experiences with Roger, in what ways did her faith provide a foundation to stand on?

14. At one point in the book, Roger says that he hates religion and all who try to explain it. Have you ever been so mad that you have questioned God and faith? Does your religion allow you to be angry with God?

15. In what ways did Roger's deployments strengthen his faith? What gives you strength through difficult times?

16. Do you think a person can be a pastor and question God at the same time? Would you want counseling from someone who was questioning God?

17. Is there a final conclusion Roger comes to concerning his faith? What conclusions do you think he has drawn, or should draw, from his experiences?